UNDERSTANDING
MARGARET ATWOOD

UNDERSTANDING CONTEMPORARY AMERICAN LITERATURE
Matthew J. Bruccoli, Founding Editor
Linda Wagner-Martin, Series Editor

Also by Donna M. Bickford
Understanding Marge Piercy

Also of Interest
Understanding Alice Walker, Thadious M. Davis
Understanding Bharati Mukerjee, Ruth Maxey
Understanding Colson Whitehead, Derek C. Maus
Understanding David Foster Wallace, Marshall Boswell
Understanding Karen Tei Yamashita, Jolie A. Sheffer
Understanding Jennifer Egan, Alexander Moran
Understanding Philip Roth, Matthew A. Shipe
Understanding Randall Kenan, James A. Crank
Understanding Stewart O'Nan, Heike Paul
Understanding William T. Vollman, Işıl Özcan

UNDERSTANDING

MARGARET ATWOOD

Donna M. Bickford

THE UNIVERSITY OF
SOUTH CAROLINA PRESS

© 2023 University of South Carolina

Published by the University of South Carolina Press
Columbia, South Carolina 29208

uscpress.com

Manufactured in the United States of America

32 31 30 29 28 27 26 25 24 23
10 9 8 7 6 5 4 3 2 1

Library of Congress Cataloging-in-Publication Data
can be found at http://catalog.loc.gov/.

ISBN 978-1-64336-446-9 (hardcover)
ISBN 978-1-64336-447-6 (paperback)
ISBN 978-1-64336-450-6 (ebook)

Dedicated to my mother R. Irene Rash whose death we still grieve. The world is a colder place without your presence. We miss you.
 July 12, 1941–August 14, 2017

CONTENTS

Series Editor's Preface   ix
Acknowledgments   xi

Chapter 1
Understanding Margaret Atwood   1

Chapter 2
The Handmaid's Tale and *The Testaments*: Dystopia Is Coming   17

Chapter 3
The Penelopiad and *Hag-Seed*: Revising the Classics   34

Chapter 4
The *MaddAddam* Trilogy: The World as We Know It Ends   51

Chapter 5
The Heart Goes Last: Desperation and Possibility   83

Notes   105
Bibliography   107
Index   117

SERIES EDITOR'S PREFACE

The Understanding Contemporary American Literature series was founded by the estimable Matthew J. Bruccoli (1931–2008), who envisioned these volumes as guides or companions for students as well as good nonacademic readers, a legacy that will continue as new volumes are developed to fill in gaps among the nearly one hundred series volumes published to date and to embrace a host of new writers only now making their marks on our literature.

As Professor Bruccoli explained in his preface to the volumes he edited, because much influential contemporary literature makes special demands, "the word *understanding* in the titles was chosen deliberately. Many willing readers lack an adequate understanding of how contemporary literature works; that is, of what the author is attempting to express and the means by which it is conveyed." Aimed at fostering this understanding of good literature and good writers, the criticism and analysis in the series provide instruction in how to read certain contemporary writers—explicating their material, language, structures, themes, and perspectives—and facilitate a more profitable experience of the works under discussion.

In the twenty-first century Professor Bruccoli's prescience gives us an avenue to publish expert critiques of significant contemporary American writing. The series continues to map the literary landscape and to provide both instruction and enjoyment. Future volumes will seek to introduce new voices alongside canonized favorites, to chronicle the changing literature of our times, and to remain, as Professor Bruccoli conceived, contemporary in the best sense of the word.

Linda Wagner-Martin, Series Editor

ACKNOWLEDGMENTS

We all have many people who have contributed to our successes and should be acknowledged. I'll begin here with thanking Linda Wagner-Martin, whose sponsorship and faith in me led to this book, and my first book, being published by the University of South Carolina Press. At the press, Aurora Bell and her staff made sure the book is a quality product and have been such a pleasure with whom to work. Thanks also to the anonymous reviewers for their feedback.

It's a commonly held understanding that academia is a small, fairly insular place. I'm not sure about that, but I do know how lucky I am to have friends, former colleagues, and former students at the institutions I've worked at who are still in my life. I've worked at the University of Rhode Island, the University of North Carolina at Chapel Hill, and Dickinson College. There are people I continue to value at all of these places. And I am so happy and fortunate to have worked with so many wonderful students during my years in the academy: I know you will do things that are important in the world.

Having the opportunity to submit this book manuscript in the spring of 2022 is a high point on which to close out my academic career, as this is the year I retired.

I am grateful to Mary Cappello, Jean Walton, and Rosie Pegueros, all of whom were significant influences in my graduate school experience, and all of whom continue to be mentors and friends. I continue to miss Dana Shugar, who passed away during my last semester of graduate school. She was a significant inspiration to me and to many others.

My two best friends, Robin Dare and Janet Hagen, are the kind of friends you can not see for years and then reconnect with as if you saw one another just the day before. Some people never have friends like this.

My late mother, Irene Rash, was always supportive and affirming of all her daughters' endeavors. I am so fortunate to have my sisters, Susan Bickford and Barbara Bickford-Wilcox, and their families as part of my life. There are many families who do not have each other's back; I'm lucky to have a family who is always there for me.

CHAPTER 1

Understanding Margaret Atwood

Thus far, Margaret Atwood has written more than sixty books, including poetry, novels, children's books, and graphic novels (one of which, the three-part *War Bears*, has been optioned for an animated series). With the recent interest in Atwood's work—the 2019 release of the Booker Prize–award winning novel, *The Testaments* (which is the sequel to *The Handmaid's Tale* and the subsequent award-winning TV series, 2017–22),[1] a graphic novel version of *The Handmaid's Tale*, the use of the Handmaids' wardrobe as a tool of protest,[2] and the 2019 release of the documentary *Margaret Atwood: A Word after a Word after a Word Is Power* (Lang and Raymont, dir.)—it seems an appropriate time to examine some of Atwood's most recent novels. In November 2021, the Canadian postal service even released a new stamp featuring Atwood. Literary critics agree that she is one of the most significant contemporary writers. In fact, Heidi Slettedahl MacPherson argues that Atwood is "amongst the most important contemporary women writers, and critics are still discovering new ways to address and respond to her work" (*Cambridge Introduction*, 120). Gina Wisker refers to her as "the greatest living Canadian writer" (*Margaret Atwood*, 1).

This volume is intended to aid readers in understanding Atwood's most recent novels by providing an overview of Atwood's life, descriptions and analyses of the key themes present in these novels, signposts to the connections and intertextual references between them, and attention to their critical reception. I hope it will help undergraduate and graduate students, as well as the general public, appreciate the wonderful depth and complexity of Atwood's work.

Margaret Atwood was born in Ottawa in 1939. Her father was a forest entomologist and Atwood spent much of her childhood living at his research sites in fairly spartan circumstances (further exacerbated by deprivations caused by World War II), but this situation was balanced by a lot of freedom to play, read, and explore. Atwood notes that because of her father's job, "I didn't spend a full year in school until I was eleven" (*Curious Pursuits*, 8), as the family oscillated between the woods and Ottawa. After the age of eleven, the family relocated to Toronto but continued to "make excursions to the northern Ontario and Quebec bush until 1961" (Rosenberg, "Who Is This Woman?" 29). Her mother worked as a dietician; with both parents in scientific careers, science was a major influence in Atwood's life early on. Atwood notes that "curiosity about almost everything" was strongly encouraged in her family (*Negotiating with the Dead*, 8).

Atwood attended the University of Toronto's Victoria College. There she studied with Northrop Frye, the famous literary critic. David Staines describes Frye as "the major figure of Canadian criticism," but of course his influence on literature and literary criticism extended far beyond Canada ("Margaret Atwood," 16). Atwood went on to attend Radcliffe College at Harvard, on a Woodrow Wilson Fellowship, where she earned her master's degree. She then began a dissertation on what she termed "the metaphysical romance" in nineteenth- and early twenty-century novels, which she ultimately did not finish (*In Other Worlds*, 9). She married her first husband, writer Jim Polk, in the late 1960s. Atwood was interviewed by writer Graeme Gibson in 1972; they were both in troubled marriages at the time (Lang and Raymont, *Margaret Atwood*). After her divorce from Polk and Graeme's divorce from his wife, she and Gibson became life partners and had a daughter, Eleanor Jess Atwood Gibson. He died in 2019. Atwood has traveled widely and lived in many places around the world in addition to Canada, including London, France, Italy, Edinburgh, West Berlin, Spain, the United Kingdom, Australia, and the United States.

In recognition of the importance of her work, the Margaret Atwood Society was formed in the 1980s.[3] The society publishes *Margaret Atwood Studies*, a journal focused on Atwood's work. Lorraine York notes that Atwood's "office interacts with this organization in order to manage information about her career" (*Labor of Literary Celebrity*, 108), although Atwood herself doesn't seem to play an active role in the society. York also commends Atwood's business acumen, noting that she presciently started her own company, O.W. Toad (an acronym of her last name), in 1976 to manage her career (*Labor of Literary Celebrity*, 99).

Atwood is the recipient of a slew of awards and accolades, including multiple Booker Prizes, a PEN Center USA Lifetime Achievement Award, the Harvard Arts medal, the British Academy President's Medal, and the Hitchens Prize, in addition to being named a member of the Order of the Companions of Honour and a Fellow of the Royal Society of Canada, among others. In a *Guardian* interview with Atwood, Lisa Allardice argues that the "central theme in Atwood's fiction is power, inequality or abuse of power, against women or anyone else" ("Margaret Atwood"). Other major themes include the environment, sustainability, and ecological devastation; corporate greed; the uses and misuses of science; and resistance. Additionally, Hadley Freeman suggests that many of Atwood's novels have a similar structure, with "one connecting thread: many of her novels are told using a retrospective narrative, with a character looking back on their former life while trying to make sense of their current one" ("Playing with Fire"). Many of the novels focus on storytelling as well, asking questions about who gets to tell what stories; whose truth is conveyed in the story; and, often, placing competing narratives in conversation with each other. Atwood herself has said that she's interested in the "unreliable nature of storytelling" and that is definitely clear in much of her fiction (Gilbert, "The Challenge of Margaret Atwood").

Atwood has also been pivotal in recognizing and claiming a distinctly Canadian literature, paying particular attention to distinguishing it from both American and British literature. In her germinal critical work, *Survival: A Thematic Guide to Canadian Literature* (1972), she analyzes Canadian authors and identifies what she considers some of the more common themes in Canadian literature. Thomas B. Friedman and Shannon Hengen note that Atwood began publishing in the 1960s, a time "when Canadian cultural and political nationalism was on the rise" ("Materials," 7). David Staines makes the connection between Atwood's career and the development of a distinctly Canadian literature even more directly: "As Atwood discovered her voice as a Canadian writer of poetry, fiction, and literary criticism, she helped the country discover its own life as a literary landscape" ("Margaret Atwood," 22). Atwood clearly cannot be pigeonholed as provincial, parochial, or regional in any way, but much of her writing is firmly rooted in the Canadian context. Howells describes Atwood as "a Canadian voice in global culture" ("Introduction," 1), but also emphasizes that "her Canadianness remains in central focus even as her global persona has evolved" ("Introduction," 2). Wisker argues that "in much Canadian writing, including Atwood's, the United States is portrayed as an invasive entity, penetrating culture, language, values, violence, and merchandising. This is not merely commercially but also psychologically engulfing, since Canadians and Americans are often elided in international consciousness" (6). It's important to note, though, that Atwood is not naively uncritical of Canada; Staines argues that her novel *Bodily Harm*, for example, "delivers a scathing commentary on her own country and its smug preferences for the security of noninvolvement" ("Margaret Atwood," 22–23).

The title of Atwood's *Survival* also gestures to a common theme in Atwood's fictional work. Many of her novels include attention to survival in different manifestations: physical survival in a harsh environment, survival of the patriarchy and the struggles against it, and the continuing survival of both colonialism and imperialism. In her *Paris Review* interview, Atwood observed that "every Canadian has a complicated relationship with the United States" (Morris, "The Art of Fiction," 72). Fellow novelist Marge Piercy notes that "her work demonstrates that a consciousness of Canadian themes has enriched her ability to manipulate them," indicating that Atwood's critical work impacts the rest of her oeuvre ("Margaret Atwood," 41).

Interestingly enough, *Survival* was published in 1972, the same year Atwood's novel *Surfacing* was published; Jerome Rosenberg argues that, although they were certainly not Atwood's first books, they "catapulted Atwood into the public eye" ("Who Is This Woman?" 31). In some ways, the novel responds to Atwood's delineation of a specifically Canadian literature by encoding anti–US attitudes in the plot. The characters consistently demonstrate anti–US sentiment, using language like "bloody fascist pig Yanks" (6) or "Yank pigs" (113). The narrator notes that "we used to think they [Americans] were harmless and funny and inept and faintly lovable," implying that she no longer thinks that (72). The narrator notes the influence of Americans on Canadians themselves, dolefully predicting that "they're what's in store for us, what we are turning into" (151). Donna Bennett and Nathalie Cooke, though, argue that Canadians "began to define and speak out of their invisibility. [Thus,] what seems simple anti-Americanism in *Surfacing* and elsewhere is more the voicing of what Canadians are not" ("A Feminist by Another Name," 35). Additionally, in both *The Handmaid's Tale* and *The Testaments*, the dystopic Gilead is set in the former United States, while those who are successful in fleeing escape to Canada, a place where they presumably seek respite from the rules and consequences of the Gileadean regime. Wisker observes that "*Oryx and Crake* is set on the East Coast of America (Atwood, with her scathing Canadian view of the US, likes to use it for her dystopias)" (*Margaret Atwood*, 147). Howells suggests this emphasizes "Canada's ambivalent relations with her southern neighbor, a situation that has become increasingly fraught since the American presidential election in 2016 and on which Atwood has become much more outspoken" (Howells, "Introduction," 4).

Wilderness is also often a theme found in Atwood's work. It figures prominently in *Surfacing*, which is set in the Canadian wilderness. Stein finds this setting important and suggests that it signifies that "wilderness (the bush), the world of nature, is an important source of values" (*Margaret Atwood Revisited*, 51). Many of the short stories in *Wilderness Tips* are set in the woods as well. Howells notes that "wilderness makes its uncanny return in the *MaddAddam* trilogy, where as a result of global warming, climate change, and a pandemic, the whole world has become a jungle" ("Introduction," 5).

Wilderness is personally relevant to Atwood as she is a lover of nature herself, as was her husband. In 2022, Atwood and the late Graeme Gibson were awarded the Douglas H. Pimlott Award from Nature Canada in acknowledgment of their important work to support nature conservation. Additionally, Atwood is a member of Nature Canada's Women for Nature initiative. Atwood and Graeme were also avid birders. In an impressive example of acting on her commitment to conservation and environmental sustainability, Atwood's O.W. Toad's office lists on its website the "Green Policies" it follows.[4] As York notes: "setting aside all of the good reasons for this emphasis on sustainability, it is also fascinating because it is one respect in which the very operations of Atwood Inc. perform the values that have been associated, since *Surfacing*, and as recently as *The Year of the Flood*, with the writings of Margaret Atwood. The office, in this way, becomes an extension of meanings engaged and explored by Atwood texts" (*Labor of Literary Celebrity*, 124).

Although this volume focuses on Atwood's recent novels, there are multiple thematic connections between Atwood's earlier novels and those discussed here. Early novels such as *Life Before Man* explore questions of extinction and survival that are revisited in *The MaddAddam Trilogy*. The influence of fairy tales and mythology can be seen in many of Atwood's novels, including *The Robber Bridegroom* (1998), which leads to the more overt reworking of myth in *The Penelopiad*. Virtually all of Atwood's novels center the stories and voices of women and attend to sexual and gender politics. And, as Karen Stein notes, "an important subject of her fiction is storytelling itself," something we'll see in many of the novels discussed here (*Margaret Atwood Revisited*, xi).

It is worth looking briefly at *Surfacing* and *Bodily Harm*, two of Atwood's early novels, before moving on to her recent ones, in order to see how themes from these early novels reappear in the later ones; Atwood's interest in certain issues has been quite consistent throughout her career. The plot in *Surfacing*, Atwood's second published novel (the first was *The Edible Woman*), centers on the search for the narrator's father; Howells refers to the novel as "a feminist quest classic" ("Critical Reception," 57). Stein, expanding on this, argues for a reading of the novel that sees it "primarily as a woman's quest and secondarily as a quest for cultural identity, describing Canada's struggle to come to terms with its past" (*Margaret Atwood Revisited*, 51). Annis Pratt suggests that the novel "has been generally accepted as an archetypal narrative dealing with a quest for rebirth and transformation" ("Surfacing and the Rebirth Journey," 139). The search for the narrator's father provides the frame through which to look at the two deteriorating and dysfunctional intimate relationships in the novel. The narrator, who is never named, is informed that her father, who lived alone in an isolated cabin near a lake in the Canadian woods, has mysteriously disappeared; she leaves the city to discover where he is. Her boyfriend, Joe, and their friends David and Anna, go with her. Her father's body is eventually discovered; the working theory is that he fell off a cliff into the lake; and he has his camera with him.

The narrator's memories of an earlier affair (although she tells Joe and the others she was married) and her abortion as a result of that sexual relationship haunt some of her thoughts. Stein argues that she "has become trapped in the story she fabricates, the story of her past that she has rewritten as a defense against her guilt because of an abortion" (*Margaret Atwood Revisited*, 43). The narrator finds a way to retell the story of her past, or tell a different story of her past, after diving into the water of the lake. Feeling "symbolically reborn through her dive, she is now able to emerge from the deathlike hell into which her guilt for a failed affair and abortion cast her" (Stein, *Margaret Atwood Revisited*, 55). The narrator then physically hides from Joe—whose marriage proposal she has declined—and Anna and David until they all leave. After her cleansing experience and their departure, she disappears into the woods for several days and then comes to the realization that "to live in this world she must make compromises with society. . . . She now plans to return to the complex, inharmonious world of society, resolving to avoid being either victim or victimizer" (Stein, *Margaret Atwood Revisited*, 55). Staines reads this as optimistic, arguing that "at the end of *Surfacing*, the woman returns to the surface, having shaken off past encumbrances and willing now to begin anew" (20). Stein, though, argues that "the book ends in a moment of stasis, balance. The lake and woods are posted in an equilibrium against Joe, who represents the city and who may be either a rescuer or an intruder" (*Margaret Atwood Revisited*, 56). Indeed, Stein's reading here seems more definitive than the actual ending of the novel, which is quite ambiguous; Joe returns to the cabin seeking the narrator, but we don't know whether she will leave with him now or continue to hide from him. A film version of *Surfacing* was released in 1981,[5] in which the narrator does return to the city with Joe. Stein concedes that "the open-ended, ambiguous published version is more fitting," and also more typical of Atwood, as "the protagonist tells and revises her quest story, but its significance and outcome are enigmatic" (*Margaret Atwood Revisited*, 57). *Surfacing* deals with gender politics, relationships, state politics, and wilderness / nature, all themes that will frequently reoccur in Atwood's works.

Bodily Harm (1982) tells the story of Rennie Wilford, a writer and journalist for a women's magazine who focuses on "lifestyle" pieces. She feels like her life is in disarray. After she has what seems to be successful breast cancer surgery, her live-in partner, Jake, breaks up with her and moves out; a mysterious man then breaks into her apartment, presumably to attack her, leaving a coiled rope on the bed when he is scared off by the arrival of the police. The police are waiting for her when she arrives home to inform her what has happened; she feels that they are implicitly blaming her for the break-in as one of them "wanted it to be my fault, just a little, some indiscretion, some provocation" (15).

After all of this tumult, Rennie approaches an editor of one of the magazines she writes for, asking for an assignment "somewhere warm and far away . . . I need some time out" (16). She is assigned to a barely known island, St. Antoine, and its sister island of St. Agathe, to do a travel piece. As Staines notes, this is "the first time she [Atwood] has moved her major fictional setting outside Canada" ("Margaret Atwood," 22) and Stein suggests that the novel's "Caribbean setting seems a radical departure for Atwood" (*Margaret Atwood Revisited*, 71). Contrary to the general perception of what being on a Caribbean island for a working vacation might be like, Rennie stays in a barely functioning hotel with tap water that is unsafe to drink, shower water that is only lukewarm, and a very limited menu. She also encounters hostile reactions from some of the locals; for example, she is told that "we don't need you here" (77). She remembers that she's "heard that the Caribbean is becoming hostile to tourists, but this is the most blatant sign she's seen of it" (77). In contrast to *Surfacing*, where Canada is portrayed as superior to the United States, here there are hints of negative attitudes toward Canada. Dr. Minnow, who Rennie meets on the plane, tells her a story about foreign aid that arrived after their last hurricane, noting sarcastically that "the sweet Canadians donated a thousand tins of ham" (29). The locals never saw the ham, which turns up on the menu at a formal banquet "for the leading citizens only. Many of us were very amused, my friend. There was a round of applause for the sweet Canadians" (29). Although the "sweet Canadians" also sent money to rebuild houses that were damaged in the hurricane, the people impacted are currently living in a tent city (125). The government has not given the rebuilding money to the people who need it. This is early evidence of the governmental corruption plaguing the island.

On the island, Rennie is befriended by two locals, Paul, who turns out to be a smuggler and who becomes Rennie's lover, and Lora. Lora used to live with Paul, but now she lives with Prince, one of the candidates in the upcoming election; she also deals drugs. When Lora asks Rennie to pick up a box at the airport for her, Rennie is immediately suspicious, but Lora assures her the box contains Prince's mother's medication. Although Rennie doesn't open the box, someone searches her room and finds it. It's unsealed when she returns to the room and she discovers it contains a machine gun. She later learns that Paul has smuggled in other guns, which are used shortly in a postelection protest.

Rennie is warned by Dr. Minnow to "be careful of the American"—in particular he means Paul (136). The hotel owner warns her about Dr. Minnow who, she says, "stirs up people for nothing" (138). Paul tells her to "stay away from Minnow," as "Ellis doesn't like him" (151); Ellis is the current Prime Minister. After Rennie starts sleeping with Paul, Lora tells her "I wouldn't get too mixed up with Paul if I was you," going on to say, "not that he gets that mixed up with most people anyway" (221). It's not clear to Rennie who she can trust or whose warning about whom might be accurate and worth heeding.

Although when Rennie sought the magazine assignment, she specified that she wants "nothing political" (16), she in fact "finds herself in the middle of a political revolution," because of the contested election between Ellis, Prince, and Minnow (Stein, *Margaret Atwood Revisited*, 71). Following the announcement of the election results, many of the local men gather and Marsden (Prince's campaign manager) incites an armed uprising against Ellis. The police pick up as many of the protesters as they can, including Lora and Rennie who are confined in the same cell.

Eventually the Canadian government arranges Rennie's release. The Canadian official tells her that "the government [of St. Antoine] can't make a public apology of course but they would like her to know unofficially that they consider it a regrettable incident" (294). He diplomatically asks her not to write about what she's seen. At first, she is outraged by the request, asking "have you any idea of what's going on in here?" (295), but as "she wants her passport back, she wants to get out" (295), she agrees. He is relieved and notes that the Canadian government doesn't "make value judgments, . . . we just allocate aid for peaceful development" (296). Staines reads this as Atwood's negative reaction to the attempt to assert an apolitical practice of international diplomacy ("Margaret Atwood," 23). The novel ends with Rennie on the plane headed home, deciding she'll return to investigative reporting, the journalism with which she started her career.

In this novel, Atwood revisits issues of state power and dysfunctional relationship dynamics, and also centers illness. Stein calls this "a new theme for Atwood" and one in which "Rennie's illness becomes a metaphor for the disorder of the body politic," thus connecting "the cancerous physical body and the corrupt and rotten body politic" (*Margaret Atwood Revisited*, 72, 77). The *Bodily Harm* of the title, then, refers both to Rennie's breast cancer and to the dysfunctional government and attempted coup in St. Antoine; it might also reference the presumably fatal beating Lora endures and possibly also the unknown intruder's plan to harm Rennie when he broke into her apartment.

Pilar Somacarrera argues that "the fictional portrait of this former British colony allows Atwood to lay bare the crudest dimensions of political power . . . the aim of absolute power is to silence *the voice*, to abolish the words, so that the only voices and words left are those of the ones in power" ("Questions of Power," 37, emphasis in the original). Having a regime determined to silence and disempower its people is a theme that also occurs in both *The Handmaid's Tale* and *The Testaments*.

In addition to her novels, Atwood is also a prolific poet. Her first published collection of poems, *The Circle Game*, was published in 1966[6] and was awarded the Governor General's Award for Poetry in 1967. *The Journals of Susanna Moodie* (1970) was inspired by Moodie's own memoir, *Roughing It in the Bush*, which was available to Atwood "in her family bookcase when she was a young girl," although Atwood didn't read it until she was at Harvard (Staines, "Margaret Atwood," 18). *The Journals of Susanna Moodie* fits squarely within Atwood's efforts to mark a corpus of Canadian literature as "she provided herself and Canadians with a literary foremother that they needed just then" (Bennett and Cooke, "A Feminist by Another Name," 33). Marlene Kadar, in fact, argues that the poems respond to the Canadian preoccupation with their status as a colony and that "Susanna Moodie is both colonizer (British) and metaphorically colonized (by the foreign wilderness)" ("*The Journals*," 148). In another poetry collection, *You Are Happy*,[7] we see an additional example of Atwood's interest in mythology, as it is about "the transformation of myth" (Levine-Keating, "Atwood's *You Are Happy*," 153). Most recently, Atwood published *Dearly* (2020), in which, Emilia Phillips says, "we see Atwood at the height of her poetic powers" ("Three of Fiction's Brightest Stars").

Charles Pachter argues that "her [Atwood's] poetry will be her most enduring legacy. I've read through her more dystopian novels, but I don't remember them the way I remember the poetry" (Isen and Viola, "The Making of Margaret Atwood," 154). Eleanor Wachtel counters by pointing out that "some people argue that they like her poetry more than her fiction, but you don't have to choose. You can have it all" (Isen and Viola, "The Making of Margaret Atwood," 154). Atwood herself describes the distinction she sees between the work of poetry and the work of fiction this way: "Poetry is the heart of the language, the activity through which language is renewed and kept alive. I believe that fiction writing is the guardian of the moral and ethical sense of the community. . . . fiction is one of the few forms left through which we may examine our society" (Staines, "Margaret Atwood," 25).

Atwood has also written collections of short stories, the first of which, *Dancing Girls and Other Stories*, includes "Rape Fantasies," a short story taught in many college classrooms. Her oeuvre includes a number of children's books, many of which "demonstrate her attitudes towards children, [and] family" (Friedman and Hengen, "Materials," 14). More recently she has ventured into graphic novel territory with *War Bears* and *Angel Catbird*. Additionally, she continues to publish updated collections of her miscellaneous writing—literary criticism, book reviews, occasional pieces, and so on. MacPherson observes that "the very fact that Atwood can package and sell her collected book reviews and occasional writing—work that is really only of interest because of its connection to Atwood-as-author suggests just how much force she has in the literary (and business) world" (*The Cambridge Introduction*, 15).

Bennett and Cook argue that Atwood's focus on Canada, which they suggest could be construed as "nationalist," functions in a similar way to feminism, because "Canadians, like feminists, have had to construct themselves out of a larger culture in which they felt invisible" ("A Feminist by Another Name," 33). Although writing strikingly feminist novels with strong female characters, Atwood has had an uneasy relationship with feminism and often resists claiming a feminist identity for herself. She has observed on multiple occasions that "I predated the women's movement, didn't create it, and didn't even participate in its early stages" and that "this has been interpreted by some as a kind of denial or repudiation," hinting perhaps at a feeling of being misunderstood (Atwood, "If You Can't Say Something Nice"). Regardless of Atwood's attitude toward the label *feminist*, there can be no doubt that she has been committed to women's equality throughout her career; her writing bears this out. Atwood continues to make comments and observations that align with feminist critiques of the patriarchy; for example, she has said, "for the female novelist, it means that certain men will find it objectionable if she depicts men behaving the way they do behave a lot of the time" and goes on to observe that if male authors write negative portrayals of men "nobody, to my knowledge, has accused those authors of being mean to men" (*Curious Pursuits*, 54, 56). She also is passionate about the power of the women's movement: "I remember a grand fermentation of ideas, an exuberance in writing, a joy in uncovering taboos and in breaking them, a willingness to explore new channels of thought and feeling" ("If You Can't Say Something Nice"). Atwood emphasizes the importance of feminism for writing: "Feminism has done many good things for women writers, but surely the most important has been the permission to say the unsaid, to encourage women to claim their full humanity, which means acknowledging the shadows as well as the lights" ("If You Can't Say Something Nice"). She also observes that one important thing the Women's Movement changed for her was that "it changed the audience"—so "people were not saying 'weird person' but they were saying, Oho, yes, right" (*Atlantis Interview*, 205).

Perhaps, as a consequence, Atwood often bristles at interview questions about gender. For example, in *Moving Targets* she writes: "I can talk about the difficulties that women encounter as writers. For instance, if you're a woman writer, sometime, somewhere, you will be asked: *Do you think of yourself as a writer first, or as a woman first*? Look out. Whoever asks this hates and fears both writing and women" (131, emphasis in original). She also alludes to the contemporary preoccupation with a writer's gender, observing that "there is, still, a sort of trained dog fascination with the idea of women writers—not that the thing is done well, but that it is done at all, by a creature that is not supposed to possess such capabilities" (*Writing with Intent*, 86). Heidi Slettedahl MacPherson, however, insists on the centrality of gender in Atwood's work, observing that "it is impossible to consider Atwood's work without considering the central importance she places on women as characters, with every one of her novels, except *Oryx and Crake*, featuring a female protagonist." MacPherson's book was written before *Hag-Seed*, which features another male protagonist (*Cambridge Introduction*, 22).

Atwood frequently teases out the political implications of her writing. When asked in a 1980 *Atlantis* interview whether her writing is apolitical, she explicitly rejects that categorization. She explains, "it's not apolitical. It's not exclusively feminist either" (*Atlantis Interview*, 205). She goes on to insist that "any writer has to resist becoming a mouthpiece for anybody—becoming a propagandist" (210), a concern she echoes repeatedly. For example, she calls out the possibility that she feels that being identified as a feminist writer might limit her in some way: "I view with some alarm any attempt to dictate to women writers, on ideological grounds, various 'acceptable' modes of approach, style, form, language, subject, or voice" ("If You Can't Say Something Nice"). As Miranda Sawyer observes, "feminism is at the root of almost everything Atwood writes, but she doesn't always toe the party line" ("'If You're Going to Speak Truth to Power,'"). This distinction echoes another caveat Atwood stresses in her work. In an interview with Rebecca Mead, she parses the distinction between exploring "questions of morality" in her work (which she does) with "avoiding moralism" ("Margaret Atwood, the Prophet of Dystopia"). This seems to be more about exploring issues and consequences, than about assigning or accepting labels.

In 2016, Atwood voluntarily stepped into a controversy over sexual harassment accusations which had been levied at Professor Steven Galloway at the University of British Columbia. She and dozens of other writers signed and published an open letter requesting that the university provide due process for Galloway, who was terminated, even though an investigation cleared him of most charges; the letter claimed that the institution had "acted irresponsibly"

("Open Letter to UBC"). There was an outpouring of protest from feminists and others, including an Open Counter-Letter by dozens of other "scholars, writers, cultural workers and allies" ("Open Counter-Letter"). In January 2018, Atwood published an opinion piece in the *Globe and Mail* entitled "Am I a Bad Feminist?" (referencing Roxane Gay's 2014 book *Bad Feminist*, although Atwood used the term in a very different way). Atwood defended herself by noting that she has always believed in "civil and human rights . . . including the right to fundamental justice" ("Am I a Bad Feminist?"). She also cited her support of the #MeToo movement, referring to it as "a symptom of a broken legal system," but insisting that transparency and accountability were important in investigating cases of sexual misconduct. Howells notes that the critics of her signing of the Open Letter "underestimated Atwood and her genuine feminist concerns, for within a few months she became one of the first funders of a new Canadian anti-sexual harassment program, AfterMeToo" ("Introduction," 5). Ultimately, though, whether she claims feminism for herself or feminism claims her, Atwood acknowledges the importance of the contemporary feminist movement as critical for women writers in giving them access to publishers and the marketplace. Her fiction consistently focuses on feminist concerns.

In 2020, Atwood unwittingly became embroiled in another charged debate. Author J. K. Rowling was widely called out for transphobia after some Twitter interactions. Rowling defended herself in a long blog entry on her website, in which she denied being transphobic, although she expressed concern about the "new trans activism" which she described as "pushing to erode the legal definition of sex and replace it with gender" ("J. K. Rowling Writes about Her Reasons"). Atwood responded on Twitter where she countered Rowling's position by sharing a *Scientific American* article called "The New Science of Sex and Gender," and arguing that science supports a more expansive and fluid version of gender than Rowling understood. Atwood followed this posting by pointing out examples of animals who don't fall within rigid gender binaries. Her support of an expansive definition of gender was foreshadowed in an earlier comment during an interview with Catherine Conroy when Atwood said she wasn't the kind of feminist "that thinks that trans women are not women" ("'When Did It Become the Norm?'").

However, almost a year later, Atwood herself was the center of a similar controversy provoked by retweeting an article written by Rosie DiManno and published in the *Toronto Star*, called "Why Can't We Say 'Women' Anymore?" in which DiManno argued (inaccurately) that by using trans-inclusive language, women were being erased.[8] The article was vociferously critiqued as transphobic, parroting the arguments of trans-exclusionary radical feminists (TERFs), and Atwood was accused of harboring similar opinions by retweeting the article. Atwood tweeted her own response, defending DiManno and claiming "Read her piece. She's not a Terf." In a February 2022 interview with Atwood, Freeman asked about her views on "the fraught modern debate over gender identity." After some back-and-forth, Atwood said flatly "I'm not going to argue about this. That's not what my book is about and that's not what we're here to discuss" ("Playing with Fire"). In a later interview, she was more resigned: "I don't care. I'm well on record of saying trans rights are human rights" (Bresge, "Margaret Atwood Worries").

Even more recently, Atwood was pulled into yet another conflict, this time not of her own choosing. In late 2021 and 2022, US school boards, legislators, and community members began efforts to remove books from libraries and school curricula that, according to the American Library Association, target "the voices of the marginalized . . . books and resources that mirror the lives of those who are gay, queer, or transgender, or that tell the stories of persons who are Black, Indigenous or persons of colour" (Armitstead, "It's a Culture War"). One of the books often targeted is *The Handmaid's Tale*. In response, Atwood notes that "they're playing woke snowflakery back: 'This might upset people'" (Armitstead, "It's a Culture War"). This is not the first time Atwood's novel has been the target of censorship. In 2006, the superintendent of a school in suburban Texas banned the book in response to a parent's complaint that the novel "was sexually explicit and offensive to Christians." After significant public comment, the school board reversed the superintendent's decision ("San Antonio Area School Board"). In an open letter in response to the news of the proposed ban, Atwood pointed out that "nowhere in the book is the regime identified as Christian" and "as for sexual explicitness, '*The Handmaid's Tale*' is a good deal less interested in sex than is much of the Bible" (Atwood, "'Handmaid's Tale'"). Atwood discussed the book bans on *Velshi on MSNBC*, noting that "your decision not to read a book is very, very different than the book being banned." (Velshi, "Prolific Author"). She went on to say that "not teaching the book in a high school is not the same as totally and completely banning it," drawing a distinction between access to the book and decisions to include it in a curriculum. The book bans continued to escalate in 2021. In response, Atwood authorized the creation of an unburnable edition of *The Handmaid's Tale*, which was sold at auction for $130,000, the proceeds going to support PEN America (Italie, "Margaret Atwood").

Much of Atwood's recent work falls within genres variously tagged as utopian, dystopian, apocalyptic, science fiction, or speculative fiction. Atwood seems willing to agree that her novels could be considered either speculative fiction or science fiction but notes the slipperiness of the terminology (*In Other Worlds*, 7, 61); she herself prefers to think of her own work as speculative fiction. The distinction, for Atwood, is that science fiction includes "things that could not possibly happen," where speculative fiction includes "things that really could happen but just hadn't completely happened when the authors wrote the books" ("Margaret Atwood: The Road to Ustopia"). Journalist Jared Bland has called Atwood "one of the best speculative fiction writers alive" ("It's 'Scary'").

Atwood notes several things that works of speculative fiction can do: "they can explore the consequences of new and proposed technologies in graphic ways, by showing them as fully operational. . . . They can explore the nature and limits of what it means to be human in graphic ways, by pushing the envelope as far as it will go. . . . They can explore the relationship of man to the universe, an exploration that often takes us in the direction of religion and can meld easily with mythology . . . [and] they can explore proposed changes in social organisation, by showing what they might actually be like for those living within them" ("'Aliens'"). These elements certainly appear in much of Atwood's speculative fiction.

However, in Ursula Le Guin's 2009 review of *Oryx and Crake* and *The Year of the Flood* in the *Guardian,* she argues that she *would* describe these novels as science fiction and suggests that Atwood resists the term "to protect her novels from being relegated to a genre still shunned" ("The Year of the Flood"), a charge Atwood denied in a 2011 piece in the *Guardian* ("Margaret Atwood: The Road to Ustopia"). Le Guin and Atwood later had a lively public discussion of this issue, among other topics, in the 2010 Portland Arts and Lectures series. When Le Guin died, Atwood penned a tribute to her, published in the *Guardian*, calling her "one of the literary greats of the 20th century" ("Ursula K Le Guin, by Margaret Atwood").

Atwood also coined a word to refer to her writing in this genre—*ustopia*—which she created by "combining utopia and dystopia—the imagined perfect society and its opposite—because, in my view, each contains a latent version of the other" (*In Other Worlds,* 66). Atwood notes that beginning with *The Handmaid's Tale*, she followed this rule: "I would not put into this book anything that humankind had not already done, somewhere, sometime, or for which it did not already have the tools" (*In Other Worlds,* 88). She often discusses the enormous amount of research she conducts for each of her novels, evidence of which is contained in her voluminous archives at the Thomas Fisher Rare Book Library at the University of Toronto.

Atwood is an active user of social media, including Twitter, where in February 2022, she had 2,012,817 followers, and Instagram, where she had 210,000. She also has a professional author's page on Facebook, which is populated and maintained by her publishers. She is a visible activist on a number of important social justice issues, including the environment, climate change, and species extinction, and is engaged with Amnesty International (a global human rights organization) and PEN International (which focuses on freedom of expression and supporting writers who are persecuted). She has also acted on television and in the theater. She had a cameo role in *The Handmaid's Tale* first season's first episode, playing an Aunt. And, more recently, she played the prophet Tiresias in the Theatre of War Productions premier of *The Nurse Antigone* on March 17, 2022 (Brall, "Theatre Review: 'The Nurse Antigone'").

The remainder of this volume will center Atwood's work by locating it in the literary, political, and social context of the latter half of the twentieth century and the beginning of the twenty-first. Chapter 2 examines *The Handmaid's Tale* (1985)[9] and *The Testaments* (2019). *The Handmaid's Tale* is eerily prescient. It is set in what was the United States and is now Gilead, a fundamentalist dystopian society based in large part on the controlling of women and exploiting and policing their reproductive capacities. The novel closes with a *Historical Notes* section, narrating an academic symposium that makes clear Gilead no longer exists. *The Testaments* is an explanation of how Gilead ceased to exist, and recounts the stories of two young girls, one growing up in Gilead and one across the border in Canada, as well as the story of a powerful female administrator within Gilead.

Chapter 3 treats two of Atwood's retellings, *The Penelopiad* (2005),[10] a reimagining of *The Odyssey* from the point of view of Penelope and her hanged maids, and *Hag-Seed* (2016), a contemporary reworking of *The Tempest* for the Hogarth Shakespeare Project. In *The Penelopiad*, Atwood revisions the story from Penelope's perspective, challenging a number of aspects of the original mythology, including calling into question the heroic stories that come to her ears about her husband Odysseus. In *Hag-Seed*, Atwood positions the director of a contemporary theater festival as the protagonist who wrestles with the changing situations in his life. The novel addresses politics and power in arts organizations, revenge, incarceration and prison education, and loss.

Chapter 4 explores the *MaddAddam* trilogy, consisting of *Oryx and Crake* (2003, shortlisted for the Booker Prize), *The Year of the Flood* (2009), and *MaddAddam* (2013). *Oryx and Crake* and *The Year of the Flood* take place in the same time period, with some characters and experiences intersecting, while *MaddAddam* begins at the chronological end of the first two novels. *Oryx and Crake* is built around the life stories of Jimmy / Snowman and Glenn / Crake. The narrative is told in flashbacks, alternating between past and present, and begins with a present moment where it appears that most of humankind has been killed by a fast-moving, horrible plague. In *The Year of the Flood*, the narrative voices focus on two women, Toby and Ren, and God's Gardeners, a small religious sect built, in part, on respect for nature. Events in these two novels are happening in parallel with each other. The final volume, *MaddAddam*, is more future-oriented, focusing less on what led to the present moment of the novel and more on how to build a life after a global catastrophe.

    The book closes with Chapter 5 which looks at *The Heart Goes Last* (2015), excerpts of which were serially published on the online platform Wattpad. This novel tells the stories of Charmaine and Stan, currently poor and homeless, who accept an offer to live at Consilience, a model town of the Positron Project. Purportedly designed to solve societal problems, Positron is an ominous example of the surveillance state, and produces resistance to its actions both from the outside and on the inside. This novel addresses a question Atwood asserts every utopia faces: "What do you do with the people who don't fit in?" (Bland, "It's 'Scary'"). Sections of the novel verge on the cartoonish (especially the enormously complicated plot to alert the outside world to what's really happening at Consilience and the use of the almost-farcical Green Men and Elvis Presley and Marilyn Monroe impersonators), but the novel also addresses deep philosophical questions about free will, population control, surveillance, desire, and love.

CHAPTER 2

The Handmaid's Tale and *The Testaments*
Dystopia Is Coming

Atwood's 1986 novel, *The Handmaid's Tale*, seems visionary. It is set in what was Cambridge, Massachusetts, which, following a takeover of the US government, has been turned into the Republic of Gilead, a fundamentalist dystopic society whose ideology is based in large part on the control of women and their reproductive capacities. Atwood explains that "stories about the future always have a what if premise" and, for *The Handmaid's Tale*, her "what if" was this question: "if you wanted to seize power in the United States, abolish liberal democracy, and set up a dictatorship, how would you go about it?" (Atwood, "Haunted").[1] She extends these questions in "Margaret Atwood: The Road to Ustopia" by asking "how much social instability would it take before people renounced their hard-won civil liberties in a trade-off for 'safety'?" She also phrases it this way: "What if it can happen here? What kind of it would it be?" ("Writing Utopia," 93). Atwood, in commenting on this novel, uses the opportunity as another moment to qualify her stance on feminism: "I wanted to try a dystopia from the female point of view.... However, this does not make *The Handmaid's Tale* a 'feminist dystopia,' except insofar as giving a woman a voice and an inner life will always be considered 'feminist' by those who think women ought not to have those things" (*Writing with Intent*, 291).

The Handmaid's Tale is one of Atwood's most popular novels thus far. Erica Wagner notes that it "was the most-read novel in the US in 2017" ("'Writing Is Always an Act of Hope,'"), and Fiona Tolan observes that it "has never been out of print" ("'I Could Say That, Too,'" 452), thus signifying its continued relevance. It was awarded the very first Arthur C. Clarke Award. It has also inspired a movie version, a wildly successful multiseason Hulu TV series, and an opera. The opera, composed by Poul Ruder, has been staged many times, beginning with a 2003 premiere in Copenhagen directed by Phyllida Lloyd, and more recently in 2022 in a version directed by Annilese Miskimmon at the English National Opera (the second time that company has staged the opera). Additionally, the Handmaid costume has been appropriated for political protest, particularly over issues related to reproductive rights. Atwood is in favor of this appropriation: "I think using the handmaids' costume as a protest mechanism is brilliant. . . . you're very visible and everybody knows what you mean" (Alter, "'I'm Too Old to Be Scared by Much'"). She notes that the costume is now part of the collection at the Smithsonian (Dudding, "Margaret Atwood").

The narrator, Offred, is a Handmaid, one of the increasingly rare still-fertile young women who have been taken from their own families and given to high-ranking Gileadean officials to mate with and bear children for their wives to raise as their own. Environmental contamination has adversely affected the reproductive capacities of most women, so those who have successfully given birth are highly desirable for their presumed ability to continue to reproduce.[2] Offred, her husband Luke, and their young daughter were caught when they tried to flee to Canada shortly after the governmental takeover. Offred doesn't know where Luke is now, or if he is even alive; she does know her daughter has been adopted by a high-ranking Gileadean family.

The Handmaids' environments are tightly controlled and surveilled. They are tattooed with identification numbers because they are considered a "national resource" (65). They are served healthy (albeit boring) food and allowed light exercise. Baths are drawn for them on a regular schedule, and their periods are tracked. They are required to do daily pelvic exercises and are taken to the doctor once a month for check-ups. Nothing is left in their rooms that they could use to hurt themselves. They are not provided with any reading materials or tasks to occupy their time other than daily trips to the market with another Handmaid companion. Offred comments on "the amount of unfilled time, the long parentheses of nothing" (69). She claims the night as "my own time, to do with as I will, as long as I am quiet" (37) and uses that time and space to remember scenes from her past. However, she tries "not to think too much. . . . There's a lot that doesn't bear thinking about. Thinking can hurt your chances, and I intend to last" (8). Offred acknowledges that, however coercive the situation was, she chose this path: "there wasn't a lot of choice but there was some and this is what I chose" (94). Other women are shipped off to the environmentally contaminated Colonies, as was Offred's feminist mother, or forced into sex work, as was her friend Moira.

After the governmental upheaval, the Aunts, older women who support the new regime, educate the Handmaids at the Rachel and Leah Center, also referred to as the Red Center, where they are housed in a dormitory, reeducated about what was wrong with the past, and instructed about their new roles. In the Red Center, Aunt Lydia lectures them on why this new system is better and on the distinctions between "freedom to and freedom from," suggesting they be glad that they now have "freedom from" harm (24). Offred thinks of all the "freedom to" she had before—to wear what she wanted, to earn her own money—but also remembers the dangers: "Women were not protected then" and could be catcalled or sexually assaulted (24). The Commander also justifies the new system to Offred, claiming it is better for women: "this way they all get a man, nobody's left out" (219). He is, however, forced to acknowledge that "better never means better for everyone. . . . it always means worse, for some" (211).

Wisker notes that "a major problem which the novel highlights is ostensible freedom—what does freedom really mean? The Aunts suggest it is freedom from (rape, sexism) rather than freedom to (do what you choose)" (*Margaret Atwood*, 90). It is clearly not freedom of movement; the Handmaids' actions and movements are highly constrained and surveilled. In addition, Gilead is clearly no example of "freedom from" sexism, as it is mired in fundamentalist, patriarchal control of women's bodies and movement and enforces rigid gender role expectations.

Women's position in society is signified by the color of their clothes. The Handmaids wear all red, "the color of blood, which defines us," with white headwear that restricts their vision "to keep us from seeing, but also from being seen" (8). The Commanders' Wives wear blue. The Marthas, house servants for those of high rank, wear green. Econowives, "the women of the poorer men" (24), wear multicolored stripes. Thus, the women's class and relationship statuses are highly visible; the clothing serves as a constant reminder of their function and, even more, emphasizes that they have value only insofar as they successfully perform that function.

The Handmaids are renamed after their Commanders and their names change if they are assigned to a new one. This is a deliberate choice and, as Elaine Tuttle Hansen observes, "serves to make it impossible to sustain female alliances—once a Handmaid moves to another posting, for example, her identity is impossible to follow" ("Mothers Tomorrow and Mothers Yesterday," 42). The reader never learns Offred's real name, but at times she says it to herself: "I repeat my former name, remind myself of what I once could do, how others saw me" (97). In the Red Center "we exchanged names, from bed to bed" (4), one of the small acts of resistance we see sprinkled throughout the novel. For Offred, her real name is power; "I keep the knowledge of this name like something hidden, some treasure I'll come back to dig up, one day" (84).

On the nights of the Ceremony, the household assembles so the Commander can read relevant biblical passages to the family and their servants. In the Commander's house, the Bible is kept under lock and key and the Commander keeps the key. Atwood comments that "in most patriarchal systems, men don't want women to read the Bible because then the men in charge can declare what's in it and no one can check up on them" (Loyd, "Dangerous Mind of Margaret Atwood"). The Ceremony itself follows the biblical story of Jacob and Rachel and her maid Bilhah, where Rachel arranges for Jacob and Bilhah to have sex so Bilhah can bear children for her. It takes place in the master bedroom, where Offred lies between Serena Joy's legs on the bed, both fully clothed except for the removal of Offred's underwear, and the Commander—also fully clothed—proceeds to have sex with Offred. She describes the mechanical, transactional nature of these encounters: "what he is fucking is the lower part of my body" (94). Serena Joy seems to resent the entire thing, tightly squeezing Offred's hands so "the rings of her left hand cut into my fingers. It may or may not be revenge" (94). Whether she resents Offred or her own infertility which makes the Ceremony necessary is not clear.

When a Handmaid is fortunate enough to conceive, the birth is a community event for women. All of the Handmaids are collected in the "red Birthmobile" (111) and the Wives in the "blue Birthmobile" (114) and they congregate at the house of the Commander where the pregnant Handmaid will give birth. Just as with the Ceremony, the Wife is ritually included in the event. During the actual birth, the Commander's Wife sits on the birthing stool above the laboring Handmaid. The other Wives are there to celebrate the birth with her. It is a rare chance for the Handmaids to share information, as long as they do so surreptitiously.

Guardians are assigned to Commanders' homes and serve as chauffeurs and assistants. Offred is suspicious of the Commander's Guardian, Nick, noticing that "he's not servile enough" (18). He also flouts the rules. As she leaves one day to do her assigned shopping, Nick winks at her. Offred is shocked and puzzled as "he's just taken a risk, but for what?" (18). When one day Nick seeks out Offred to tell her the Commander wants to see her, he unexpectedly kisses her (98), another risk. The purpose of taking these risks is unclear. What does Nick hope to gain? Offred does note that Nick must have "low status" as "he hasn't been issued a woman, not even one" (18), but Nick doesn't seem motivated by desire. The instruction for Offred to appear before the Commander alone is quite unusual, as Commanders are not to interact with their Handmaid except "for breeding purposes" (136). Offred is nervous, but she cannot really refuse the Commander's summons. This moment marks a change in the dynamics of their relationship, however. If they are discovered, she will be punished more severely, but there will be consequences for him, too. Offred realizes that now she has some small power and "can ask for something. Possibly not much, but something" (144).

Offred is surprised when she learns that he wants to play Scrabble with her, a pastime that is no longer permitted. Women are not allowed to read, so the game itself is "forbidden" and "dangerous" (138). At the end of the evening, he asks her to kiss him, to kiss him "as if you meant it" (140). The secret trysts continue and during her time in his study, Offred is permitted to look at old magazines under the Commander's watchful eye and apply hand lotion, a cosmetic the Wives have banned. In fact, the Handmaids are permitted no cosmetics or beauty aids, because "they don't want us to look attractive. For them, things are bad enough as it is" (96). Offred finds this new access to language and the written word almost seductive. One night, the Commander provides her with some revealing clothes and makeup and Nick drives them to Jezebel's, a secret club where other high-ranking men are interacting with sex workers. The Commander says that some of them were prostitutes before but others "prefer it here, too" (238). When Offred asks "prefer it to what?" the answer is unsatisfying: "to the alternatives" (238). Offred is surprised to see that her friend Moira is one of the women. They meet in the restroom where Moira tells Offred how she got to Jezebel's. She was caught trying to escape Gilead and, as the Commander said, was given the choice to go to the contaminated Colonies and clean them up (probably a death sentence) or to Jezebel's. She chose Jezebel's because "shit, nobody but a nun would pick the Colonies" (249). At the end of the evening, the Commander takes Offred upstairs to a hotel room for sex. She finds this difficult because, "usually, I'm inert" during the Ceremony, and mentally urges herself to "fake it, . . . let's get this over with or you'll be here all night" (255).

After several months, frustrated that Offred has not conceived, the Commander's Wife Serena Joy makes her an unusual offer, suggesting that she have sex with Nick. Offred is reluctant to agree because of the risk, but Serena Joy notes that she "might as well" (206), implying that if Offred doesn't get pregnant, there will also be unpleasant consequences. Offred knows this is true and thus agrees to the arrangement. The same night the Commander takes her to Jezebel's is the night Serena Joy has selected for her assignation with Nick. After their first encounter, Offred continues to visit him at night without Serena Joy's knowledge. This, too, is dangerous, but Offred notes that she is "beyond caring" (270). Hungry and desperate for an authentic human connection,

Offred shares some of her past with Nick and tells him "things I shouldn't," including her real name (270).

Offred tries to compartmentalize her current situation from her inner self. When she refers to her bedroom, she thinks of "the door of the room—not *my* room, I refuse to say *my*" (8). And, after returning from the market, she encounters the Commander in the hallway "near the door to the room where I stay" (49). Offred can't imagine why he is there but, after he leaves, she wonders, "was he in my room? I called it *mine*" (49). There seems to be a need for her to claim possession when there is the possibility that the Commander has entered or violated her space.

After exploring the room carefully when she first arrives, primarily as a way to pass the time, Offred finds words scratched into the closet: "*Nolite te bastardes carborundorum*" (52). This small discovery confirms for her that there had been other Handmaids in the Commander's house before her. She later discovers that it means something like "don't let the bastards grind you down" (187), an apt message of encouragement for one Handmaid to be passing on to another.

The Gileadeans have not forgotten the importance of ritual. In addition to the Ceremony, there are Prayvaganzas, Salvagings, and Particicutions. The Prayvaganzas are public group marriages of Angels who have been rewarded for their service with daughters from important families. They are also, Offred says, a chance to "demonstrate how obedient and pious we are" (212). They are always gender-segregated spaces; the only men present seem to be Guardians, the Angels being married, and the Commander performing the wedding. The women are segregated as well—the wives in seats and the Handmaids standing behind a rope to signify their lower status; it also, Offred notes, "keeps the others from contamination by us" (214). Salvagings are public hangings for those who have committed crimes. Again, the women are separated: the wives are seated toward the back and the Handmaids kneel on cushions at the front. Aunt Lydia presides over this one and, early in the event, tells the audience that although they used to share "a detailed account of the crimes of which the prisoners stand convicted, they've decided not to as, when they do, it seems to always be followed by an "outbreak . . . of exactly similar crimes" (275). The Handmaids are disappointed at this news as "the crimes of others are a secret language among us. Through them we show ourselves what we might be capable of" (275). At this Salvaging, Offred witnesses two Handmaids and a Wife put to death. This one is followed by a Particicution, where the Handmaids are permitted to physically attack and kill a Guardian who has been convicted of rape (279); it was designed so that "it would also act as a steam valve for the female elements in Gilead" (307).

Throughout the novel, there are frequent acts of resistance, albeit small ones, enacted by the Handmaids. On a visit to the market, Offred allows a young Guardian to make eye contact with her, "a small defiance of rule, so small as to be undetectable, but such moments are the rewards I hold out for myself . . . such moments are possibilities" (21). The Handmaids hide the butter they are given with meals to use on their skin. Offred sees this as belief in a future, noting that "as long as we do this, butter our skin to keep it soft, we can believe that we will some day get out, that we will be touched again, in love or desire" (96–97), rather than serving as a brood mare. She also hypothesizes—or perhaps hopes—that "there must be a resistance, a government in exile" (105). In a bit of foreshadowing, when her market companion Ofglen once comments on the nice May day, Offred remembers that "*Mayday* used to be a distress signal." In the earlier times, Luke told her it comes from French "From *m'aidez*. Help me" (44). It is much later when Ofglen tells her that the password for the resistance, which does exist, is Mayday (202). Although Offred learns little about the resistance until the very end of the novel, Slawomir Kuźnicki observes that Mayday is not just working to overthrow the regime, but perhaps modeling a new way to organize society, as "Mayday is an organization founded and maintained by both men and women, which may suggest that only cooperation of the two sexes can result in gender justice and equity" (*Margaret Atwood's Dystopian Fiction*, 2). This analysis makes clear the way that Mayday is organized stands in clear and direct opposition to the separate spheres practices of Gilead itself.

When Serena Joy discovers Offred's trysts and outing with the Commander, she is furious. Offred knows there will be consequences but, when the black van of the Eyes comes for her, she realizes "worse is coming" (293). Nick whispers to her that it is Mayday, using her real name as code to convince her to believe him. She's not sure she can but, again, she really has no choice. Offred assumes Serena Joy called them, but when Serena Joy asks, "what has she done?" Offred realizes that "whatever she had in store for me, it was more private" (294). The Mayday Eyes say it is for "violation of state secrets" (294). As Offred steps into the van, she notes that, "whether this is my end or a new beginning I have no way of knowing" (295). Her story ends on this inconclusive note.

Offred's delivery to the black van is followed by a (fictional) *Historical Notes* section, narrating the proceedings of an academic symposium that makes clear that although Gilead no longer exists, Offred did survive and managed to record her story; VanSpanckeren calls this a "tricky ending" ("The Trickster Text"). York suggests that this section is "entirely about the way in which all texts are mediated by those who produce and reproduce, publicize, translate, or edit them" (*Labor of Literary Celebrity*, 164.) A self-important male scholar, Professor Pieixoto, shares the events that led to the discovery of Offred's tapes. In a stunning moment of uncritical cultural relativism, he warns the audience about "passing moral judgment upon the Gileadeans," insisting that "our job is not to censure but to understand" (302). Ultimately, he is disappointed in the content of Offred's tapes, as "she could have told us so much about the workings of the Gileadean empire" (310), instead of the story she did tell. For example, he wants to know which Fred she was attached to; the choices among senior Gileadean officials are "Frederick R. Waterford and B. Frederick Judd" (306). Wisker argues that Pieixoto's critique of the choices Offred made in her historical narrative "serves as an example of male intellectual control over history" (*Margaret Atwood*, 87). Tolan suggests that "by juxtaposing his remote intellectualism with the immediacy of Offred's 'I,' Atwood undermines his position by demonstrating how it disregards her [Offred's] suffering" (*Margaret Atwood,* 169). Kuźnicki also defends Offred's narrative choices, noting that she is "a narrator that is far from being omniscient, and yet becomes the only source of information, not only about her inner thoughts and feelings, but also about the external world of the regime that surrounds her" (*Margaret Atwood's Dystopian Fiction,* 32). In fact, Offred can only tell the story she tells: "as she repeatedly says . . . she does not know any version that is whole and original," if, indeed, such a version exists (Hansen, "Mothers Tomorrow and Mothers Yesterday," 39). Atwood herself explains her narrative strategy by arguing that "it would be cheating to show the reader more than the character has access to. Her information is limited. In fact, her lack of information is part of the nightmare" (Penguin Random House, "Interview with Margaret Atwood").

One review of *The Handmaid's Tale* criticizes Atwood's choice to end with this appendix, arguing that it "seems an unnecessary blunt, even cruel, way to end such an astonishing narrative" (Lewis, "*The Handmaid's Tale*"). Lorraine York suggests, in contrast, that this postscript, "is broadly representative of her [Atwood's] lively concern for the ways in which art is produced and mediated (*Labor of Literary Celebrity,* 164). We might add that texts are also mediated by those who discover them, as Pieixoto makes clear. Additionally, the postscript is where we learn a little about Offred's presumed escape from Gilead and Gilead's destruction, providing the closure that Offred's own narrative cannot offer.

Indeed, this novel is also about the power of narrative. Offred tells her story, narrating her life and memories throughout the novel. This, too, is an act of resistance and requires faith that there is someone who will listen. As Offred points out, "you don't tell a story only to yourself. There's always someone else" (40). Tolan observes that what Offred does "is to create an audience for her narrative when no such audience exists" (*Margaret Atwood*, 172) and finds that "the metafictional status of Offred's tale is founded in the self-consciousness of her storytelling and the self-reflexivity of her narrative" (*Margaret Atwood*, 169). Wisker argues that Offred's "habit of talking about storytelling highlights the processes of constructing and representing histories and legitimated or repressed versions of events" (*Margaret Atwood*, 95), implicitly positioning Offred's choices positively against Pieixoto's criticism. Atwood herself has described Offred's actions as part of a "literature of witness" and "an act of hope" (Atwood, "What 'The Handmaid's Tale' Means").

Decades after *The Handmaid's Tale*, Atwood published a follow-up novel. *The Testaments* (2019) relies on the earlier novel but is not exactly a sequel. Atwood has shared in multiple interviews about *The Testaments* that she resisted writing a sequel to *The Handmaid's Tale* because "reinhabiting the voice of heroine and modern-women-turned-sex-slave, Offred . . . was, for her, an impossibility" (Loyd, "Dangerous Mind of Margaret Atwood"). The question that drove this second narrative, Atwood says, is that "totalitarian systems don't last . . . when they come apart, what is it that causes them to fall apart?" (Alter, "'I'm Too Old to Be Scared by Much'"). Robin Young also notes that the novel explores "why do collaborators collaborate?" ("'It's Creepily Similar'"). Through the character of Aunt Lydia, this question becomes one of the central narrative arcs of the novel. In an interview with Atwood, Gilbert contrasts this novel with *The Handmaid's Tale*, arguing that "if *The Handmaid's Tale* is all about Offred's passivity and powerlessness, *The Testaments* is defined by action. Its characters find power in unlikely places" ("The Challenge of Margaret Atwood"). The critically well-received *The Testaments* was awarded the Booker Prize in 2019.[3] MGM TV and Hulu decided to move forward with a TV series before the book was even available publicly. Tajia Isen and Daniel Viola suggest that prior to the release of *The Testaments*, Atwood was known as "a perennially prizewinning, bestselling author" ("The Making of Margaret Atwood," 153). However, they claim, after the publication of the book, she became "a worldwide cultural phenomenon" (153).

The Testaments occurs several years after *The Handmaid's Tale* and is the explanation of how Gilead ceased to exist. It recounts the stories of two young girls, Agnes and Daisy, one growing up in Gilead and one across the border in Canada, both of whom—we learn much later—are Offred's daughters. In fact, as Loyd notes, "the question of who their mother is propels the story, as do the girls' voices" ("Dangerous Mind of Margaret Atwood"). The other narrative voice is that of Aunt Lydia, who was one of the Aunts who trained and controlled the handmaids in *The Handmaid's Tale*. She is the only character common to both novels (except for a brief appearance by Offred, whose real name turns out to be June). In *The Testaments,* Lydia is extremely powerful for a woman in Gilead and is placed in charge of Ardua Hall, a religious convent of sorts. Atwood suggests that "Aunt Lydia's always been a climber, so she climbed up" (Alter, "'I'm Too Old to Be Scared by Much'"). She is also a mole, one of the central contributors to the eventual success of the Mayday resistance to the Gileadean regime. The portrayal of Aunt Lydia's character in *The Testaments* differs significantly from her portrayal in *The Handmaid's Tale.* In part, this may be that her years in Gilead have impacted her, moving her from begrudging acquiescence to complicity to resistance. Or she may have always been subtly resisting but biding her time until she gained enough power for more consequential action. However, in *The Handmaid's Tale,* we only see Aunt Lydia from Offred's point of view, so it is difficult to know.

As does *The Handmaid's Tale,* this novel functions as a metanarrative about storytelling, as the characters often comment on the possibilities and reactions of their future audience, as well as reflecting on the choices they make about what to tell and when. The novel emphasizes the importance of testimony and witnessing, both of which assume "the presence of a future reader" (Gilbert, "Margaret Atwood Bears Witness"). *The Testaments* in fact begins with Aunt Lydia's direct address to "my unknown reader," followed almost immediately by her pessimistic speculation that "perhaps I will never have a reader" (5). Later she asks: "Who are you, my reader? And when are you?" (62). Agnes's and Daisy's narratives are framed as Witness Testimony and appear to be relayed orally (as does Offred's) in real time to unidentified others. Agnes begins in response to a prompt: "you have asked me to tell you what it was like for me when I was growing up within Gilead" (10). Daisy invokes similar language: "you've said that you'd like me to tell you how I got involved in this whole story" (39).

In this novel, we have the opportunity to "see Gilead from within, from without—and from a founder" (Wagner, "'Writing Is Always an Act of Hope'"). It is here that we learn Aunt Lydia's backstory. Formerly a family court judge, she is arrested after the attack "that liquidated Congress" (66). Along with other professional women, she is taken to a stadium where they are held for some time in subhuman conditions and forced to witness other women being executed. Eventually, Lydia is brought to see Commander Judd and is asked to cooperate with the new regime. When she prevaricates, she is imprisoned in solitary confinement and tortured. She eventually agrees to cooperate and is assigned, with three other women, to "help us to organize the separate sphere—the sphere for women" (175). Sophie Gilbert observes that Lydia's narrative primarily "focuses on the suffering she endured, not the suffering she meted out" ("Margaret Atwood Bears Witness"). Gilbert argues that this novel makes "a more loaded demand than its predecessor did—that readers place themselves in the seat of an oppressor, not one of the subjugated" ("Margaret Atwood Bears Witness"). Amy Grace Loyd describes this novel as "alive with the contradictions of a woman who's a player in a power structure that also subordinates her" ("Dangerous Mind of Margaret Atwood"). Michiko Kakutani affirms that Lydia is "a survivor, someone who's done what she thinks necessary to avoid death or further loss" ("The Handmaid's Thriller"). As Atwood herself notes, people like Lydia "want to climb up the ladder. Keep the power. In regimes like that you don't get fired. You do or die. Frequently both," perhaps hinting at the untenable position in which Lydia finds herself (Loyd, "Dangerous Mind of Margaret Atwood").

Complicating Gilbert's claim about suffering, however, Lydia frequently does consider the moral consequences of her actions and decisions. In fact, she is "well aware of how you must be judging me, my reader" (32) and acknowledges that, in part, writing her story is about "defending my life . . . the life—I've told myself—I had no choice but to lead" (36). Anticipating judgment, she imagines the reader asking, "how can I have behaved so badly, so cruelly, so stupidly? You will ask. You yourself would never have done such things!" But Lydia goes on to point out that "you yourself will never have had to" (403). Aviva Dove-Viebahn suggests Lydia's actions "provoke a crucial question: What would you give up to survive? Your friends? Your family? Your humanity?" ("True to Life," 40). In *The Testaments*, Lydia serves as "a chronicler of Gilead who in some sense challenges both Offred's appraisal of her and the reader's" (Gilbert, "The Challenge of Margaret Atwood").

Dove-Viebahn argues that "Aunt Lydia's greatest fear seems to be not that she will be forgotten, but that her truths will be left untold" ("True to Life," 40). Lydia herself notes her "larger fear: that all my efforts will prove futile, and Gilead will last for a thousand years" (278). She muses to herself about whether she is "the Recording Angel, collecting together all the sins of Gilead" or whether she is "merely a dealer in sordid gossip" (278), leaving this question for readers to decide.

In Agnes's story, we have an insider's view of the regime. Agnes is the daughter of the high-ranking Commander Kyle and his wife, Tabitha, but we learn almost immediately that she is adopted (12). In a moment that takes us back to Offred's memories of trying to escape Gilead with her husband and daughter, Agnes remembers that "I did have a hazy memory of running through a forest with someone holding my hand" (12), leading us to wonder who that someone might have been. The Marthas also make a comment about "her mother" with the implication that it is someone other than Tabitha, which confuses her (21). Later her friend Shunammite tells Agnes that her "real mother" was "stealing you from Gilead," something she must have overheard her own parents discussing (84–85).

Agnes is being socialized into her future position as a Commander's Wife primarily by a series of Aunts, other girls at school, and the Marthas at home. The Aunts focus on the importance of purity, modesty, and propriety, along with justifications of why men were more important than women: women "had smaller brains that were incapable of thinking large thoughts" (15). The girls at school share rumors and gossip and any knowledge they think they have. For example, Shunammite tells them that babies come out of stomachs (23) and that "a slut was a woman who'd gone with more men than her husband" (80). Vera, Rosa, and Zilla, Kyle and Tabitha's Marthas, educate Agnes about her future duties—she'll have Marthas to do the housework and, if necessary, a Handmaid to do the shopping.

After Tabitha dies, Kyle remarries and arrangements are made for Agnes to be married. She is taken out of school, given a new wardrobe, and sent to Rubies Premarital Preparatory where the girls are to learn "how to act as mistresses of high-ranking households" (161). Her childhood friends Becka and Shunammite are there as well. Eventually both Becka and Agnes appeal to be accepted into Ardua Hall as supplicants as a strategy of marriage resistance. Deirdre Raftery cites the historically accurate practice of turning to the convent as a way to avoid marriage; it was not uncommon because "religious life allowed them [nuns], irrespective of education or wealth, to escape the drudgery of married life and childbirth" ("Rebels with a Cause," 733). It is also one of the only alternatives.

Unlike other women, the supplicants are taught to read and write. Once they have achieved a sufficient level of literacy, they are allowed into the Library and later into the more private and restricted Reading Room. After they are able to read the Bible for themselves, Becka and Agnes learn that they had been lied to by the Aunts about what the biblical teachings actually say and what they mean. Agnes realizes that she "had not seriously doubted the rightness and especially the truthfulness of Gilead's theology," but now that she had access to the Bible for herself, all of that is called into question (303). Atwood has observed that "in most patriarchal systems, men don't want women to read the Bible because then the men in charge can declare what's in it and no one can check up on them. They're in charge of the word of God" (Loyd, "Dangerous Mind of Margaret Atwood"). That was certainly true in *The Handmaid's Tale*, and Agnes has discovered that it is true in her life as well.

Agnes is engaged in copying Aunt Lydia's speeches when she mysteriously gains access to a substantial amount of new information, which leads her to further doubt what she's been told all her life. Folders with the actual circumstances of various events are left for her by an unknown person—including information about her father and her stepmother, as well as her intended husband Commander Judd. Agnes acknowledges that "once a story you've regarded as true has turned false, you begin suspecting all stories" (307). She also recognizes the many possibilities of having access to more knowledge once she becomes an Aunt: "all of the secrets I had learned, and doubtless many more, would be mine, to use as I saw fit. All of this power" (309). One of the secrets she learns, through her anonymous benefactor, is that her biological mother and father are Mayday operatives, and she has a half-sister—Baby Nicole, who is currently in Canada.

In addition to Lydia's and Agnes's insider perspectives, we also see Gilead from the outside. Daisy is brought up in Canada, the daughter of storeowners Neil and Melanie. When Daisy is helping in their store, *The Clothes Hound*, she encounters the Pearl Girls, missionaries from Gilead who distribute brochures intended "to lure you to Gilead," as well as propaganda about "Baby Nicole," a child purportedly taken from her Commander father by her Handmaid mother and smuggled into Canada. Baby Nicole, an icon, is "practically a saint in Gilead" (45); in Canada, she seems to symbolize resistance to the Gileadean regime.

Daisy suspects that there is something not quite right about her family situation; her parents "were too careful around me, as if I was breakable" and Melanie "didn't smell to me like my mother" (47). There are no pictures of her as a child (47), which she also finds puzzling. Her parents' intense concern for Daisy is evident when her class at school is taken to a protest march; Daisy is not permitted to go because "it's not safe" (49), but she finagles her way onto the bus anyway. Baby Nicole is used as a symbol at the protest but, in opposition to Gilead's portrayal of her as kidnapped, she is a symbol of freedom: "ALL GILEAD BABIES ARE BABY NICOLE" reads one of the protestor's signs (51). The implications of this slogan are not completely clear, but it hints at the need to liberate other Gilead babies. Daisy appears in news coverage of the protest, which causes significant consternation at home. Shortly after the march, *The Clothes Hound* is broken into and robbed, and then bombed; her parents are killed. It seems clear that there is a connection between Daisy's visibility at the protest and her parents' death. What is not clear is who is responsible and why.

And, yet, perhaps the timing is coincidental. The news of Neil's and Melanie's death is relevant in Gilead, as Commander Judd tells Aunt Lydia that they have "succeeded in identifying and eliminating two of the most active Mayday operatives" (63). Aunt Lydia's Pearl Girls "pointed the way" (64). Aunt

Lydia describes them as "observant, well-trained, and obedient"; in fact, they were her idea because in the past, "other missionaries had gathered information used in espionage, so why not ours?" (64). However, it is clear to Judd that the operatives "must have had a counterpart here in Gilead," someone of fairly high rank with "access to our security personnel deployments" (65). Aunt Lydia uses this information with other senior Aunts to consolidate power and suggests treachery: "if you notice anything suspicious—anything, by anyone, even anyone at Ardua Hall—do let me know" (114). In this way, she continues her strategy of keeping the other women pitted against each other; "divide and conquer could be my motto" (177). If the other women are suspicious of each other and try to curry favor with Lydia, her power and control is reinforced.

More information is discovered about the Mayday activities in which Melanie and Neil were involved. It appears that messages were being sent between them and their mysterious conspirator in Gilead by means of microdots. The mechanism is later explained to Daisy: the microdots were hidden in the brochures the Pearl Girls distributed (without their knowledge). Neil had a microdot camera to read the messages and send responses back; the camera was destroyed in The Clothes Hound robbery, as was the "Upstate New York escape route" (297). The one remaining thread of hope for the success of the resistance is the Gilead contact who Mayday has deduced must be "one of the Aunts" (203). That person had promised "a very big document cache" and apparently has a strategy for getting it to them that involves Baby Nicole (197).

After her parents' death, Daisy is told the truth about her past. She is younger than she was told; Melanie and Neil were not her parents but were part of Mayday; her actual parents are still alive; she was born in and smuggled out of Gilead; and she is, in fact, Baby Nicole. Mayday determines that Baby Nicole could enter Gilead without detection by pretending to be converted by the Pearl Girls and could then make contact with the informant once she is able to find out who it is. Daisy agrees to participate in the undercover operation and changes her clothes and appearance before she is sent out to the streets, now as Jade, to be scooped up by the Pearl Girls. She is successful in infiltrating Ardua Hall, and Becka and Agnes are assigned to acclimate her to its routines and customs.

Once all of Lydia's arrangements to transfer her information via Nicole are in place, she has a moment of self-doubt, wondering whether she would go ahead with her plan to begin the destruction of Gilead, or whether she will allow the regime to use Nicole for their propaganda purposes, further cementing her "control over Ardua Hall" (317). Agnes encounters similar moral dilemmas, balancing her desire to have access to the information the Aunts have, which gives them power, with some concern about "all of this potential to judge the wicked in silence, and to punish them in ways they would not be able to anticipate. All of this vengeance" (309). But, despite these qualms, she is "tempted" (309).

After Lydia decides to go forward and transfers the information she's collected to Daisy / Jade / Nicole, Nicole must return to Canada. The strategy is the reverse of the deception that helped get her out: she will go with Agnes on a Pearl Girl mission. Aunt Lydia makes the necessary arrangements and the girls' journey into Canada is accomplished through a number of cars, trucks, buses, and boats organized by the Mayday network. After a treacherous and unplanned final dinghy trip, they make it to land and meet Ada, Garth, and other Mayday operatives, including their mother.

As the deceptions that allowed their escape begin to unravel at Ardua Hall, Lydia comes to terms with the fact that she will ultimately be held accountable: "there is scant chance I myself will escape unscathed from the revelations that are sure to follow once Nicole appears on television news in Canada and the cache of evidence she is carrying for me is displayed" (392). Lydia writes these, her last words, to her future reader before the Eyes come to take her away.

As in *The Handmaid's Tale*, *The Testaments* is layered with moments of resistance and rebellion, small and large. Gilbert notes that "its characters find power in unlikely places" ("The Challenge of Margaret Atwood"). As an important actor in the leadership of Gilead, Aunt Lydia has some books that are "off-limits to the lower ranks" and compiles intelligence, "the secret histories of Gilead," to make "profitable in non-monetary ways" (35)—presumably to retain and gain power and to keep herself "safe" (62). This information includes activities by the Commanders, their wives, other Aunts, and the supplicants.

The Testaments closes in the same way as *The Handmaid's Tale*, and it is in this final section that we learn the purpose of Agnes's and Daisy's witness narratives. Professor Pieixoto is presenting again at another Symposium on Gileadean Studies, this time about *The Ardua Hall Holograph*, which he authenticates as being written by Aunt Lydia, and the testimonies of Agnes and Daisy which, he speculates, were "recorded and transcribed most likely for the use of the Mayday Resistance movement' (412). We learn that Daisy, Agnes, and the release of the information they carried out of Gilead sparked "a popular revolt" and was "instrumental in initiating the final collapse of Gilead" (411). Kakutani suggests that "Nicole, Agnes and, yes, Lydia are leaving behind accounts that will challenge official Gileadean narratives" ("The Handmaid's Thriller"), echoing what we saw in *The Handmaid's Tale*, the continuing battles over who gets to tell which histories and which histories are memorialized.

In these novels, Atwood treats Serena Joy and Lydia with sensitivity as she explores their passive and active complicity with the Gilead regime. Prior to Gilead, Serena Joy is a public figure, making speeches "about the sanctity of the home, about how women should stay home" (45), which she, of course, is not doing at that time. In Gilead, she is now without a public role or even much freedom of movement. Offred speculates about "how furious she must be, now that she's been taken at her word" (46). The relationships between the Wives and Handmaids are often strained. During their indoctrination, Aunt Lydia asks the Handmaids to sympathize with the Wives: "try to think of it from their point of view . . . it isn't easy for them" (14) and "of course they will resent you" (46). In fact, when Offred arrives at her current posting, Serena Joy instructs her: "I want to see as little of you as possible" (15). Offred observes that "she doesn't speak to me, unless she can't avoid it. I am a reproach to her; and a necessity" (13). Although we learn of Lydia's complicity and her concern about being held accountable by future readers for her decisions from her own words, we only see Serena Joy's actions through Offred's eyes. But Atwood helps the reader understand what Serena Joy and Lydia experience and why they might have made the choices they've made, while simultaneously marking them at fault in supporting the regime for their own benefit and to protect their limited scope of power at the expense of others. This reckoning is similar to what Gloria Anzaldúa writes about in *Borderlands/LaFrontera*, when she holds Chicanos to account for their violence against women: "Though we 'understand' the root causes of male hatred and fear, . . . we do not excuse, we do not condone, and we will no longer put up with it" (83). Thus, readers may come to understand, and maybe even sympathize with, Serena Joy's and Lydia's decisions and choices and the need to make them, but we cannot justify or excuse those decisions and choices. In many ways, this reflects the central argument of Atwood's essay, "Spotty-Handed Villainesses," in which she defends an author's choice to portray female characters with a full range of emotions, experience, and motivations, whether negative or positive.

In both novels, we also see Lydia and Offred relying on the performance of acceptable femininity as a way to signal at least surface compliance with the expectations of the patriarchal power structure. This pretense at compliance is strategic, tactical, and necessary since it functions as a survival mechanism. The women have limited choices in their current situations, choices that don't differ that much from the choices produced by the expectations and demands of current patriarchal systems, which find various ways to punish women who do not act in ways that are deemed appropriately feminine. Both Lydia and Offred use the façade of femininity to hide their emotions and thoughts.

In *The Handmaid's Tale* and *The Temptations*, we encounter the founding of Gilead and its subsequent destruction. After the publication of *The Testaments*, Atwood commented frequently about the similarities between the novels and the political consequences of the 2016 US presidential election in which Donald Trump was elected. The border between the United States and Canada plays an important role in both novels and in reality; after the 2016 election and the pandemic, "Americans are sneaking into Canada to escape their own country's hopeless approach to Covid-19 . . . the woods are being watched for escapees" (Sawyer, "'If You're Going to Speak Truth to Power'"). And as in the novels, Atwood considers the impact of having and using power unwisely: "often, it goes to people's heads, . . . whoever is 'winning,' through privilege or popularity, will take it out on others" (Sawyer, "'If You're Going to Speak Truth to Power'"). These novels both offer a rich and full portrayal of multiple aspects of power—power over, patriarchal power, fundamentalist power, power struggles between women, the power of resistance, and more—in ways that resonate deeply with contemporary readers.

CHAPTER 3

The Penelopiad and *Hag-Seed*
Revising the Classics

The Handmaid's Tale and *The Testaments* highlight who gets to tell which stories and how they are told; this chapter focuses on two novels in which Atwood rewrites canonical works, thus claiming the right to reimagine these stories. *The Penelopiad* is a retelling of the *Odyssey* and *Hag-Seed* is a retelling of *The Tempest*. In this, Atwood joins a tradition of female writers who have provided new versions of some acknowledged classics.[1] Although these are very different stories, deception is a significant theme in both—deception of the world, deception of others, deception of self.

The Penelopiad (2005)[2] was written for the Canongate Myths Series, a series which, the Cannongate Books website says, centers "bold retellings of legendary tales, by the world's greatest contemporary writers." In writing about her creative journey to *The Penelopiad* for the series, Atwood observes that "strong myths never die. Sometimes they die down, but they don't die out. . . . But myths can be used—as they have been, so frequently—as the foundation stones for new renderings that find their meanings within their own times and places" (Atwood, "The Myths Series and Me"). Elodie Rousselot argues that Atwood's new version of the myth "questions some of the fundamental assumptions made in the mythical narrative" and accordingly creates "a specifically female historical space in which traditionally oppressed female figures are given an opportunity to make themselves heard" ("Re-Writing Myth," 131). In this "new rendering" of *The Odyssey*, Atwood centers female voices and female agency as "the authority of the male voice, Homer's voice, is challenged and the gaps in the original myth are identified and filled by a feminine narrative" (Rousselot, "Re-Writing Myth," 138). Susanna Braund names the novel "herstory" and notes that Atwood "demythologizes mythology" ("'We're Here Too,'" 202).

Like *The Handmaid's Tale* and *The Temptations,* this novel is driven by Atwood's questions: "what led to the hanging of the maids, and what was Penelope really up to?" (*The Penelopiad*, xv). Atwood's re-imagining, told from the point of view of Penelope and her dead maids, is also about the art of storytelling: Who is the narrator? Which narrators have agency and control of their story and when? Which version of the story can be trusted? Wisker points out that the novel "continue[s] Margaret Atwood's fascination with storytelling and the fictionalizing process" and that Penelope "reveals the plots and fictions which kept her and her court busy, her myth intact" (*Margaret Atwood*, 132). It's a very postmodern approach, challenging the notion of reliance on a universal truth or master narrative. Gerardo Rodríguez Salas notes that "not only does she [Atwood] provide an alternative image of the myth of Penelope, but she concentrates on the storytelling process to generate an alternative tradition of women's writing" ("'Close as a Kiss,'" 22). Atwood herself suggests that "Penelope's opening speech presupposes an audience" (Atwood and Lloyd, "She's Left Holding the Fort"), a supposition which echoes the concern of the protagonists in both *The Handmaid's Tale* and *The Temptations,* each wondering if anyone will ever hear their stories. Penelope herself, though, notes that "most of the time I have no listeners, not on your side of the river" (4).

Atwood suggests that the book is "a lot like the structure of a Greek tragedy" (Atwood and Lloyd, "She's Left Holding the Fort"). Penelope tells her story in short chapters interspersed with chapters from a chorus of her maids, who are "given an important narrative role" in this version, unlike in the original (Rousselot, "Re-Writing Myth," 131). The multigenre chapters in the maids' voices include both prose and verse, as well as a play, a pseudo-lecture, and a courtroom scene. Rousselot suggests this "unconventional narrative structure . . . destabilizes Homer's ancestral myth" ("Re-Writing Myth," 132) and, further, is a version "distinct even from Penelope's version" (139), again raising the question of which version to believe or, indeed, whether we can believe any of them. As Atwood discusses in her Notes at the end of the novel, she did indeed model the maids' chorus on "the use of such choruses in Greek drama" (198). The original purpose of the Greek chorus, Kelly Hishon states, "was to provide background and summary information to the audience to help them understand what was going on in the performance. They commented on themes, expressed what the main characters couldn't say (like secrets, thoughts, and fears) and provided other characters with information and insights ("Exploring the Greek Chorus").

Penelope takes charge of her story posthumously from Hades, where she encounters other characters from the *Odyssey*, also dead. She describes the different levels of Hades, disclosing that "I don't frequent the really deep levels much" (16); it is in the deep levels where the more gruesome tortures are imposed. She also talks about the permeable barrier between Hades and the world. Inhabitants of Hades can "go on an outing" (17) when they are summoned to prophesize for mortals; they can appear in their dreams; or they might be called by sorcerers and magicians. Penelope "never got summoned much by the magicians"; they overlook her to favor Helen, her beautiful cousin (20).

Penelope immediately challenges the accuracy of the version of the story told in *The Odyssey*, pointing out that "many people have believed that his [Odysseus'] version of the story was the true one" (2). She implies, however, that his version is not accurate. She also acknowledges her own complicity in allowing Odysseus that power: "I didn't ask awkward questions, I didn't dig deep. I wanted happy endings in those days" (3). She now rejects that version of herself: "And what did I amount to, once the official version gained ground? . . . A stick used to beat other women with. Why couldn't they be as considerate, as trustworthy, as all-suffering as I had been?" (2). Sophie Gilbert observes that "Atwood exposes the many ways that reputation management can influence testimony: Penelope, as Atwood portrays her, chafes at her long-suffering image" ("Margaret Atwood Bears Witness"). In Atwood's novel, Penelope also rejects the version of herself that others are circulating, because they "were turning me into a story, or into several stories, though not the kind of stories I'd prefer to hear about myself" (3). Ultimately, Penelope insists on claiming narrative agency for herself: "it's my turn to do a little story-making" (3). In her "story-making," Penelope makes clear the flaws and inaccuracies in all these other descriptions of herself. However, these multiple and competing narratives mean that, even at the end of *The Penelopiad*, we don't have a clear sense of the most reliable or accurate way to understand Penelope and her actions.

As the daughter of a king and a Naiad (a water nymph), Penelope's marriage is arranged. She describes the transactional nature of marriage for women like her. Penelope understands her role as a potential wife; her marriage will not be about love and romance. Rather, marriage is about inheritance and the acquisition of property. She notes that "marriages were for having children, and children were not toys and pets. Children were vehicles for passing things along," such as "kingdoms, rich wedding gifts, stories, grudges, blood feuds" (24). In her father's court, the "ancient custom" of contests to determine the successful suitor is followed (26); the contest for her hand is a running race which Odysseus wins. At her wedding, Penelope reminds us again of the commercial nature of the event, noting that "I was handed over to Odysseus, like a package of meat.... A sort of gilded blood pudding" (39), a commodity.

Penelope is a clear-eyed realist. Although people attempt to flatter her or ingratiate themselves by remarking on her beauty, she acknowledges that "they had to tell me that because I was a princess" (21). She knows that she "was nothing special to look at," but she is proud that she is "very smart" (21). She is also "a kind girl" (29). Odysseus is also considered clever and, according to the maids, probably "too clever for his own good" (31). Her cousin, Helen of Troy, points out with her normal superior tone that "they say he's very clever. And you're very clever too, they tell me. So you'll be able to understand what he says. I certainly never could" (34). Thus, Helen implies, Odysseus wasn't an appropriate suitor for Helen herself. Penelope reads this comment as a reminder that she "was at best only second prize" (35).

Despite the reality of the motivation for her marriage, Penelope and Odysseus appear early on to find happiness. On their wedding night they trade stories about their youth and, Penelope observes, "by the time morning came, Odysseus and I were indeed friends" (48). However, even at this moment of connection, Penelope doesn't lose her ability to face the truth, noting that "I myself had developed friendly feelings towards him—more than that, loving and passionate ones—and he behaved as if he reciprocated them. Which is not quite the same thing" (48).

One of the threads running throughout the novel is the deep jealousy between Penelope and Helen of Troy, her cousin; it's a relationship that reinforces societal beliefs that women are naturally competitive, particularly over men. Salas notes that "In the rivalry between Penelope and her cousin Helen of Troy, Atwood shows how patriarchy promotes enmity among women as a way to keep them under men's control and not to form a solid coalition" ("'Close as a Kiss,'" 26).[3] It's not only that Penelope resents Helen's beauty (although Penelope does refer to her as "intolerably beautiful") or the way men are drawn to her, or that Helen always "wanted all the attention for herself," even in Hades (33). It is also that Helen consistently insults and undermines Penelope. Penelope finds Helen's viciousness painful, noting that "her lightest sayings were often her cruellest" (33); she herself can generally find no appropriate response to Helen's comments. The animosity continues even after they are both dead. In one exchange in Hades, Penelope encounters Helen on her way to bathe although, as Penelope points out, "spirits don't have bodies" (153), clearly seeing this act as Helen taking the opportunity to gain male attention. Helen uses the moment to complain that "divine beauty is such a burden" and to sneer at Penelope, "at least you've been spared that!" (154).

We see similar backbiting and undercutting between women once Odysseus takes Penelope to Ithaca, his home. Penelope's mother-in-law, Anticleia, is less than pleased with her son's marriage and although she greets her new daughter-in-law appropriately, it is clear to Penelope that "she didn't approve of me" (60). In fact, Penelope thinks that Anticleia "would have been better pleased if I'd died of seasickness on the way to Ithaca and Odysseus had arrived home with the bridal presents but not the bride" (62). Penelope must also contend with her husband's "former nurse, Eurycleia" (60) who does help acclimate Penelope to the customs of her new court and is "at least friendly" (62) in comparison to Anticleia. But she also disempowers Penelope by insisting on tending to Odysseus and leaving Penelope herself "no little office I might perform for my husband" (63). Eurycleia often undermines Penelope's efforts, telling her no matter what she did or how she did it that "that wasn't how Odysseus liked things done" (63). Although Penelope eventually feels a bit more at home, she feels frustrated because she "had little authority within it [her new home], what with Eurycleia and my mother-in-law running all domestic matters and making all household decisions" (71).

In a chapter entitled "Helen Ruins My Life," Penelope discovers even more justification for her dislike of Helen. When Paris, son of King Priam, falls in love with Helen and they run away to Troy together," Odysseus and the other men are forced to honor a prior oath and "wage war to get Helen back" (78). This war is the reason Odysseus is gone from Ithaca for years, and, eventually, for many suitors to arrive seeking Penelope's hand in marriage. Over time, it becomes obvious that "hope had dwindled and was flickering out" (103) for Odysseus's return, and it is increasingly likely that he is dead. Here again we see Penelope's candid assessment of herself in comparison to the flattery the suitors are expressing: "they punctuated their drunken parties and merrymaking with moronic speeches about my ravishing beauty and my excellence and wisdom" (104). Eating her out of house and home and sucking up her son Telemachus's inheritance, the suitors "said they would continue in this manner until I chose one of them as my new husband" (104). Penelope complains that "month by month the pressure on me increased" (109). Although she tries to resist them with a reminder "that the eventual return of Odysseus had been foretold by an oracle" (111), it does no good. The suitors escalate their pressure, becoming even more demanding, and Penelope is eventually forced to invent a delaying tactic: she claims she can't marry until she has woven a shroud for Laertes, Odysseus's father. Every day she weaves and every night she and her maids unravel her progress, thus buying her time.

The suitors also have a negative impact on her relationship with Telemachus. Penelope begins to notice that "he was starting to look at me in an odd way, holding me responsible for the fact that his inheritance was being literally gobbled up" (109), since she could presumably decide to remarry and preserve it. Additionally, Telemachus is coming into maturity and is "now of an age to start ordering me around"; he also "wanted to assert his authority as the son of Odysseus and take over the reins" (121). In one attempt to prove himself, he sneaks away on a ship to try to ascertain what happened to his father. Penelope is distraught, even more so when she discovers that the "interfering old biddy Eurycleia . . . had aided and abetted him" (122). The suitors arrange for "a ship of their own to lie in wait for him and ambush him and kill him on his return voyage," but Telemachus returns unharmed after avoiding the murder attempt (122). When Penelope scolds him, Telemachus responds by asserting his rights and accusing Penelope of not acting appropriately: "he didn't need anyone's permission to take a boat that was more or less part of his own inheritance, but it was no thanks to me that he had any inheritance left, since I hadn't defended it and now it was all being eaten up by the Suitors" (128). Eurycleia joins in, calling Penelope a "crosspatch mummy making him all sad" (130).

Penelope has to find ways to respond to all of these complicated situations. In Atwood's revisioning, Penelope strategically attempts to navigate the changing political landscape and the multiple competing interests of those who surround her. Encouraging her maids to spy on the suitors as a way to get information (having sex without their owner's permission is the "crime" for which they are ultimately hanged), she collects useful tidbits and context. She also offers alternate interpretations for some of the heroic stories that she hears about her husband; did Odysseus battle "a giant one-eyed Cyclops" or was it really a "one-eyed tavern keeper" who wanted payment of a bill (83)? Penelope also recognizes Odysseus when he returns in disguise and can see that Telemachus is aware of the deception as "his shuffling and stammering and sideways looks gave him away" (137). Penelope assumes Odysseus properly "appraised the situation in the palace" and knew that if he simply arrived and ordered the suitors out, "he'd have been a dead man within minutes" (136). However, she pretends not to know who he is and proceeds to stage an archery contest that she knows only he can win, thus enabling him to reclaim his kingdom.

Penelope's relationships with her maids serve multiple purposes. They are her servants, but they are also her "sources of information" (30) about any number of things. Because they serve (and sleep with—or are raped by) the suitors, they are privy to conversations that Penelope is not. Additionally, Rousselot notes that the evenings where Penelope and her maids are unraveling her weaving "amount to scenes of celebration" ("Re-Writing Myth," 137); they share stories, jokes, and delicacies, and the hierarchies that govern the maids' behavior during the day seem less important. In a way, these experiences serve to level the otherwise-asymmetrical power between Penelope and her servants (although that doesn't protect them from death when Odysseus returns). Penelope describes their relationships in these moments as "almost like sisters" (114). For most of the novel, the maids and Penelope are joined together against patriarchy and otherwise trying to resist unequal gender relations. Their bonding stands in strong contrast to the competition between Helen and Penelope and even between Penelope and Eurycleia, but, ultimately, this female unity is called into question.

In "The Chorus Line" chapter, the maids reconstruct an earlier conversation between Penelope and Eurycleia as the two, worried that the maids will disclose Penelope's infidelity in Odysseus's absence, plot the maids' murder. In the maids' version, Penelope has indeed been unfaithful to Odysseus and Eurycleia promises to arrange their deaths to protect her. Rousselot observes that "through the insertion of a play acted by the maids, Atwood suggests that Penelope had in fact been promiscuous with the suitors and that it was she who had ordered the maids to be hanged because they knew her secret" ("Re-Writing Myth," 140). After Penelope learns that the maids have been murdered by Odysseus and Telemachus, she, horrified, blames herself. In this version, Penelope wonders whether if she had told Eurycleia of her instructions to the maids to spy on her behalf, their murders could have been avoided? She acknowledges that her decision, though, was "in hindsight, a grave mistake" (115). However, in contrast, part of her believes that Eurycleia did indeed understand the actual situation and acted "out of resentment at being excluded and the desire to retain her inside position with Odysseus" (161). Readers never learn the truth about Penelope's alleged infidelities or the depth of Eurycleia's knowledge.

The death of the maids does benefit Penelope in some ways. In this framing, the maids' deaths are what enables Penelope to become "a symbol of wifely loyalty and chastity" (Rousselot, "Re-Writing Myth," 134)—an image she later resents, but one which protects her reputation and status in the moment of Odysseus's return.

In an attempt at accountability, Odysseus is put on trial for the murders of the suitors, a charge which is ultimately dismissed. The maids are furious that he is being tried only for the suitors' murder and that their deaths are being ignored and demand that the judge punish Odysseus for their murders, crying "we demand justice! We demand retribution!" (183). Penelope is called to testify and claims she was asleep, both when the maids were raped and when they were hanged. When the judge asks her if she believed they were raped, she responds with a qualified yes: "That is, I tended to believe them" (181), thus sending a subtle signal that their description of what happened might be suspect or, at least, that she may not wholly believe it. In contrast to Penelope's mixed messages, Braund argues that Atwood "insistently and compellingly presents their experience of fraternizing with the suitors as rape and their subsequent hanging as unjustifiable—and she indicates Penelope's responsibility for their deaths" ("'We're Here Too,'" 202). And, of course, the maids' murder is a perfect example of Atwood's definition of politics: "Politics, for me, is everything that involves who gets to do what to whom" (Somacarrera, "Questions of Power," 32).

The novel ends with the maids' voices as they haunt those who murdered them and those who permitted the murderers to go free. The maids suggest that these guilty actors "should have prayed for our forgiveness" (192) and go on to suggest that their vengeance will never end: "we'll never leave you, we'll stick to you like your shadow, soft and relentless as glue" (193). In fact, when Odysseus visits Penelope in Hades, the maids' presence is extremely disconcerting to him. Penelope understands that "they make him nervous. They make him restless. They cause him pain. They make him want to be anywhere and anyone else" (189). Seeing the maids forces Odysseus to remember what he did to them. Although the maids "not only roundly criticize Odysseus for hanging them but also explicitly hold Penelope responsible for not preventing their deaths," their haunting presence apparently doesn't have the same effect on Penelope herself (Braund, "'We're Here Too,'" 205).

The reader is left with no way to determine who is telling the truth or ascertain the accuracy of any version of the multiple stories related in the novel. As Penelope herself says, she and Odysseus were both "proficient and shameless liars of long standing" (173), raising doubts about the accuracy not only of his claims, but also of hers. In fact, Braund describes Penelope as "not a reliable narrator" ("'We're Here Too,'" 204). Sudha Shastri notes that the impact of these competing stories "complicates the whole idea of a feminist voice, because when there is more than one woman telling her story, what happens when their stories are at odds with one another?" ("Revisi(ti)ng the Past," 147). The novel does not answer this; there is no real resolution, and we are left to try to make sense of the competing narratives ourselves.

In Atwood's retelling of another canonical work, *Hag-Seed*, the female voice is replaced with a male narrator, a rare occurrence in Atwood's work as was noted with *Oryx and Crake* (in fact, thus far only two Atwood novels have male protagonists). This novel is a volume in the Hogarth Shakespeare Project which, according to the publisher's website, "sees Shakespeare's works retold by acclaimed and bestselling novelists of today." Atwood's contribution is *Hag-Seed* (2016), an updated version of *The Tempest*. Paul Joseph Zajac argues that "although references to Shakespeare's plays appear throughout Atwood's writing, *Hag-Seed* certainly marks her most concerted engagement with the Bard" (326) and that it "is not just a celebration or critique of *The Tempest*, but a reflection on the very project of adaptation" ("Prisoners of Shakespeare," 339). Staines insists that it is a "perfect example of a first-rate writer adapting, updating, and extolling the profound merits of Shakespeare's late play" ("Margaret Atwood," 28).

Of her decision to retell *The Tempest*, Atwood shares that "it was my first choice, by miles. It contains a great many unanswered questions as well as several very complex characters, and the challenge of trying to answer the questions and tease out the complexities was part of the attraction" ("A Perfect Storm"). Consistent with her motivation in writing other novels, as Atwood makes clear, the motivation for *Hag-Seed* is also the questions it raises. She comments that "Shakespeare is infinitely interpretable" and concludes her essay about writing the novel by observing that "writing Hag-Seed was strangely invigorating, and also very informative" ("A Perfect Storm").[4]

The book was well-received by literary critics. Coral Howells asserts that "Atwood is reinterpreting Shakespeare for a new generation; *The Tempest* remains central, for her novel retains the dramatic five-act structure and Shakespeare's plot elements" ("True Trash," 309). Readers will notice other similarities to the original play as well. Howells reads *Hag-Seed*, in part, as Atwood's invoking "the powers of theatrical fantasy to create an imaginative escape within prison walls" ("True Trash," 313). Viv Groskop refers to the novel as "something extraordinary" and describes it as "riotous, insanely readable and just the best fun" ("*Hag-Seed* Review," 2016).

The novel is an imaginative mash-up of genres including narrative, ghost story, revenge plot, playscript, and rap lyrics. It begins by bringing the reader into a truncated screening of a performance of *The Tempest* by the Fletcher Correctional Players before moving on to tell us the backstory of Felix Phillips. A widower whose three-year-old daughter Miranda died a few years after his wife, he is famous as the director of the Makeshiweg Festival, a summer theater program. This career choice is clearly a gesture to *The Tempest*; Atwood notes that "of all Shakespeare's plays, this one is most obviously about plays, directing and acting" ("A Perfect Storm"). Felix is summarily fired by his Board, purportedly over his avant-garde plans for staging *The Tempest*; the message is gleefully delivered by his devious, power-grabbing assistant Tony Price. Over the years, Felix has delegated all the parts of his job he doesn't like to Tony, thus allowing Tony to consolidate power and influence and successfully pull off the coup. This sequence of events parallels the ousting, in *The Tempest*, of Prospero, the Duke of Milan, by his devious brother Alonso; as Atwood observes, "Prospero's loss of his dukedom is largely his own fault—by his own admission, he neglected to take care of his realm" (Atwood, "A Perfect Storm"). Felix recreates himself as Felix Duke (another nod to Shakespeare, alluding to the Duke of Milan) and takes up residence in a ramshackle cottage. After a period of "mourning and brooding" (38), he realizes that he "required a focus, a purpose" (41) and decides both that "he needed to get his *Tempest* back" and that "he wanted revenge" (41). The two are not mutually exclusive and he accomplishes both simultaneously.

At the same time, he begins daydreaming about Miranda, his dead daughter, imagining what she would have been like as she grew up. Howells suggests that in this way, Atwood "transforms Shakespeare's father–daughter relationship into a ghost story" ("True Trash," 310). Atwood, in fact, has referred to Miranda as "the spirit-girl" ("A perfect storm"). Felix begins to feel as if "she was still there with him, only invisible" (45). Even though he knows it's not true, he "engaged in this non-reality as if it were real" (45). Merry Lynn Byrd suggests that "in his grief, Felix turns Miranda into his muse and his guide" ("Maybe the Answer Was Miranda All Along," 76). Although she died as a child, she appears to him as the age she would have been had she still been alive. He reads books to her, shares meals with her, teaches her to play chess. Returning home one day, he doesn't feel her presence. He reminds himself "she was never here. It was imagination and wishful thinking . . . Resign yourself. He can't resign himself" (109). He projects feelings onto Miranda, noting that she "doesn't like it when he's depressed" (110). She pouts; she's moody; he feels her "sulking on her bed, as teenage girls do" (173). Thus, the novel portrays one example of a parent's reaction to losing a child and, in particular, a young child. There's no chance for the child to actualize its potential. Zajac argues that "this spirit-Miranda doubles as a compensatory fiction and an indication of Felix's tenuous grip on reality" ("Prisoners of Shakespeare," 326); he goes on to suggest that "his relationship with spirit-Miranda . . . exposes the extent to which his daughter's death possesses him" (330), implying that his deep grief is producing this hallucination. Interestingly enough, however, when he was running the Makeshiweg Festival, even after her death, he never felt her presence. Possibly he intentionally kept himself constantly busy as a way to avoid confronting his loss.

Felix does know that "she did not exist. Or not in the usual way" (47), but one day he hears Miranda singing. This aural hallucination unsettles him, leading him to wonder if it occurred because he is alone so much. This awareness motivates him to take a job at the Fletcher County Correctional Institute in its Literacy through Literature program to provide himself with more human contact.[5] The program was designed by Estelle, a professor who continues to supervise it and obtain government funding to run it. When they meet for the interview, she is clearly attracted to Felix. Felix thinks "now that she'd accepted him for the job, she was relaxed enough to flirt" and proceeds to warn himself "don't start anything you can't finish" (52).

Felix begins to teach Shakespeare to the incarcerated men, staging one play each spring. He develops his teaching method, which remains consistent for all the plays. The men read the text (along with Felix's summary of the plot and a glossary he's prepared for its "archaic words" (56); they discuss the meaning of the play; they study the main characters and their motivations; they rehearse and perform the play (it's recorded for screening to the entire prison); and finally, they create an afterlife for the character they played. In a clever aspect of his method, the actors compile a list of the curse words from whatever play they're studying; they are permitted to use only those curse words during the time they are working on the play. From *The Tempest*, for example, they pull out "scurvy awesome," "way to red plague go," and "poisonous poxy" (101–102).

Atwood sets her novel in a prison as "there are a lot of them [in *The Tempest*]. In fact, every one of the characters is constrained at some point in the play" (Atwood, "A Perfect Storm"). When he chooses *The Tempest* as the next play they'll do, Felix also identifies prison as one of the themes of the play. He makes a competition of having his actors find the number of prisons in the play; they come up with eight. He notes that there are really nine and promises to disclose the last prison after they've done the play. Emily St. John Mandel approves of Felix's choice of play, noting that "in some ways, staging the play at the prison is an elegant choice: Prospero's island is both prison and theater, and the play-within-a-play was of course a favorite device of Shakespeare's" ("Brave New World"). Zajac suggests that Felix's "efforts to narrate and work through trauma are mediated by *The Tempest*, and his traumatic suffering is both expressed through and exacerbated by his relationship to Shakespeare's work" ("Prisoners of Shakespeare," 324).

The novel focuses little on prison operations or prison culture outside of Felix's classroom. Of course Felix goes through the appropriate security screenings when he is at the prison, although the guards seem respectful, and there are some prohibited items he cannot bring inside. When he introduces *The Tempest* to his actors, there is outright refusal to play Ariel, "a fairy" (88), or Miranda; the actors are "not being a girl, either" (88). Felix understands this, knowing that the expectation of machismo in the men's prison would make these choices unacceptable and make his actors vulnerable: "any man playing her [Miranda] would lose status in a disastrous way. He'd become a butt, a target. Playing a girl, he'd risk being treated as one" (88). Instead, he hires Anne-Marie Greenland, his earlier choice for Miranda in the Makeshiweg version, as his Miranda for this performance. Felix does share the actors' backgrounds and conviction records with Anne-Marie, feeling that she has a right to know with whom she's working (143). Somewhat intrigued by the idea that a young woman will be joining the cast and coming into their group in the prison, the actors are placated. However, there continues to be fervent resistance to the notion of playing Ariel. In fact, there is downright refusal: "not playing a fairy, that's final. Like I said" (102). Felix understands what they are thinking, "too weak. Too gay. Out of the question" (102). In fact, when he thinks about "Ariel's song that claims he sucks like a bee, forget it: who with any sense of self-preservation would sing that?" (102) (although by the end, they do use the song, changing the words to *"where the bees buzz, there buzz I"* (245, emphasis in original). To address the actors' resistance to playing Ariel, he talks them through a redefinition of the role. First, Felix outlines his Ariel's characteristics: "First, he can be invisible. Second, he can fly. Third, he has superpowers, especially when it comes to thunder, wind, and fire. Fourth, he's musical. . . . Fifth: *he's not human*" (104). Now the men are interested, talking about the possibilities in this new way of looking at the character. They finally decide that Ariel should be portrayed as an alien superhero. Then Felix plays his trump card: "Ariel performs the single most important act in the whole plot, because without that tempest there's no play. So he's crucial. . . . So, he's like a digital expert. He's doing 3-D virtual reality" (106). Now the men are completely on board and the opposition to playing Ariel has melted away. Felix claims the role of Prospero for himself.

His ghostly daughter, Miranda, becomes interested in being in the play and wants to play Miranda. In this request, we see that perhaps Miranda also feels the loss of her potential because of her early death. And why wouldn't she prefer to be in the play instead of entertaining her father with chess games or aimlessly drifting around the cottage? Felix, reasonably, refuses this request. He thinks "how to tell her that no one but he himself would be able to see her?" (173). But when he is rehearsing his lines at home, "he hears his Miranda's voice" (185), responding to his cues with Ariel's lines and it becomes clear to him that she is "understudying Ariel" (185). Although invisible, she makes her presence known; other people hear her too. When 8Handz, Felix's Ariel, is saying his lines, he hears something "like someone was saying the lines at the same time as me" (195); Felix believes this was Miranda. On the actual night of the show, she appears as "a glimmer behind 8Handz' left shoulder" (215) and later as "a shadow, a wavering of the light" (238). When Felix and 8Handz are cleaning up after the play, 8Handz hears singing through his headphones; the disembodied voice is singing "Merrily, merrily, merrily, merrily, Life is but a dream" (245). Felix knows it's Miranda because he used to sing that song to her when she was little.

The theater in jail program is hugely successful: it improves the prisoners' literacy scores significantly, and it is also popular with them. In recognition of its success, a ministerial visit is arranged; the delegation includes Lonnie Gorgon, chair of the Makeshiweg Festival Board; Tony, who has managed to get himself appointed as Minister of Heritage; Sebert Stanley, Minister of Veterans Affairs; Sal O'Nally, Minister of Justice; and Sal's hapless son, Freddie, currently an intern with the festival. This visit provides Felix with an opportunity to design and enact his revenge on his nemesis, Tony, as well as on those who were complicit in Felix's ouster. He decides to use the performance of *The Tempest* for the occasion.

Felix relies on Shakespeare's original plotline to design his strategy: "Prospero is a director. He's putting on a play, within which there's another play. If his magic holds and his play is successful, he'll get his heart's desire" (118). To achieve his goal, Felix, too, will stage a play within a play. This complicated revenge arrangement is a testament to Felix's skill as a director, both in the creation of the double play and also in motivating his actors. In tandem with rehearsing *The Tempest*, Felix has designed an intervention for the distinguished visitors and has been rehearsing "the secret directions" with his actors (205). In actuality, "there will be not one play performance but two running simultaneously, the official one and its dark double" (Howells, "True Trash," 311). Felix relies on one of the prisoners, 8Handz, to assist with the special effects; 8Handz is in prison because of computer hacking. Felix refers to him variously as "a boy-genius hacker" and "genius black-hat hacker" (84–85). Atwood, in fact, has asked: "after all, what is Ariel but a special effects man?" ("A Perfect Storm"). Atwood's description makes it into the prison play almost verbatim; as Felix notes to the actors, "if he were here with us now, he'd be called the special-effects guy" (106).

Felix convinces his actors to participate in the deception he's planning by sharing the news which he has learned from Estelle—the politicians want to cancel the Literacy through Literature program; Felix is planning to use the politicians' reactions to the "dark double" experience as a way to get leverage and keep the program functioning. He assuages Anne-Marie's concerns about the second play, reminding her that one of the ministers "crapped up your career twelve years ago" (207) by canceling Felix's earlier *Tempest*. In still another parallel with Shakespeare, Felix replicates Prospero's desire and ability to manipulate people and events. St. John Mandel finds the willingness of the prisoners to participate in this plan completely suspect. She argues that "these are inmates in a medium-security prison, who are being asked to menace two federal ministers. They've been told the literacy program is in peril, but this alone can't explain why they'd risk longer sentences, deferred parole or transfer to maximum security for such a harebrained scheme." It's a fair point. St. John Mandel hypothesizes that it might be because they are "under the wizard's [Felix's] spell ("Brave New World").

At one moment during rehearsals, Felix faces a minor mutiny. SnakeEye, playing Antonio, complains about one of Felix's soliloquies. In Act I, Scene 2, Prospero tells of "Prospero's doleful history" (159), providing the audience with Propero's backstory. The Antonio team objects to this, saying "It's too long, . . . Plus it's boring" (159). In his own mind, Felix agrees, reflecting that the "scene's been a challenge for every actor who's ever played Prospero," but he also tells SnakeEye why it's important: "the audience needs to know the information, . . . Otherwise they can't follow the plot" (159). SnakeEye acknowledges this but also says his team has come up with a solution. With Anne-Marie's help, they've composed a rap song to tell Prospero's story. Felix has to acknowledge that "it has something" (163), but also feels that the men are "cutting me out" (159) so that SnakeEye has devised "a bigger part for himself" (160). Still, he realizes that his jealousy is inappropriate: "it's their show, he scolds himself" (163). He agrees to the substitution.

Felix has arranged for the ministerial visitors to watch *The Tempest* video with the actors in the rehearsal room. Everyone else will watch it upstairs, "on the closed-circuit TVs," as is the normal routine (72). One of the actors escorts the visitors from the prison screening area, explaining to them that they will be experiencing "an interactive piece of theatre, experimental in nature" (212). The video starts and, at the end of the Prologue, Felix's alternate play begins. Rather than the shipwreck which precipitates much of the action in *The Tempest*, here the catalyst is the façade of a prison riot. The power goes off, the video stops, and shots are heard. The lights are off; the music is loud; the actors reappear in intimidating costumes. Freddie is separated from the others and another shot is heard. He is taken to a cell, where Anne-Marie arrives to coach him through the next phase of the deception. Freddie is completely enthralled by her and, by the end of their time in the cell, it is clear that they are drawn to each other. Byrd notes this as another similarity to the original *The Tempest*: "Just as in the original, they fall in love over a game of chess—this time during the prison performance of *The Tempest*" ("Maybe the Answer was Miranda All Along," 79). The other visitors are taken hostage and confined in another jail cell. Sal is convinced that Freddie has been killed because he's not confined with them and shots were heard. With the assistance of 8Handz's contacts on the outside, Felix has purchased some illegal drugs to administer to the delegation—some to make them sleepy and some to cause hallucinations and disorientation. Freddie is not drugged. Although the others have been dosed with some of the same drugs, only Sal and Lonnie are given the sleep-inducing ones. This leaves Tony and Sebert awake and able to talk with one another, which gives Felix the opportunity to take advantage of "a rivalry between the two of them" (201).

After being convinced that Lonnie and Sal are asleep, Tony initiates a conversation with Sebert about their political prospects. He then proceeds to admit to orchestrating Felix's termination from the festival and leveraging his influence to replace Felix. Tony then assures Sebert of his own support in the upcoming election. He goes on to observe that "a couple of hundred of years ago we would take advantage of the chaos and dispose of Sal, and blame it on the rioters" (227), going on to acknowledge that they'd also have to get rid of Lonnie. With these actions, their own chances of advancement would improve. Sebert is shocked and Tony quickly backpedals, claiming the suggestion was just a "thought experiment" (228), although he has detailed the possible means of the murder: they could drown Sal in the toilet and smother Lonnie with a pillow. Tony does not know that Felix is recording the entire conversation.

Now that the visitors are completely terrified, the cell door mysteriously swings open and they carefully make their way back to the rehearsal room where refreshments, including the drugged grapes, are arranged on the table. All of them eat some except Lonnie. A small speaker has been planted on him in the middle of all the tumult, and he is warned not to eat the grapes. There is more loud music and intimidating special effects; Sal, Tony, and Sebert begin to hallucinate. They are in such bad shape that 8Handz objects, saying, "this is too sick even for me, . . . It's beyond a bad trip, they're scared shitless" (237). With some light pressure from Miranda (she notes that if she were human, she would feel sorry for them), Felix determines that "that's enough vengeance" (238); he has the visitors brought back to the main room where they had earlier been watching the video. They soon recognize Felix and he lays out his demands: he wants his job back at the Makeshiweg Festival and he wants a guarantee of at least five more years of funding for the prison literacy program; Tony is to resign; Sebert will "back out of the [political] leadership race" (241); and 8Handz, who has helped Felix with all the special effects and the drugs that he administered, will receive an early parole. As inducement (i.e., blackmail), he shares that he has their recent damning conversation on video and reminds them that "none of you would want this to go viral on the Internet" (241). Freddie is reunited with his father and the others, and then Freddie announces that he and Anne-Marie are now partners. (Fear can certainly bring people together, but this seems remarkably sudden.)

Zajac argues that "the execution of Felix's revenge arguably shows him at his least sympathetic, even if none of his marks are physically harmed. Given his reaction to the death of Miranda, Felix's leading Sal to think his son Freddie has been killed comes off as particularly callous" ("Prisoners of Shakespeare," 335). St. John Mandel agrees, finding this aspect of the revenge plot very troubling, noting, with concern, that "in at least one aspect, convincing an adversary his son has died, the viciousness is magnified exponentially by the fact that Felix knows what it's like to lose a child." She also acknowledges that when Felix "activates his plot and traps his enemies in a psychedelic hell of an interactive theater experience, he believes his revenge is justified" ("Brave New World"). In a counter-reading of this aspect of the plot, Byrd argues that "ultimately, Felix seeks justice, not just punishment" ("Maybe the Answer Was Miranda All Along," 77). She goes on to suggest, though, that "as he achieves all that he desires, Felix finds that he is no longer driven, making Atwood's revision very clearly about restitution and restoration rather than revenge" (77). The ghostly Miranda also encourages this interpretation. While he's driving home from the performance, Felix thinks: "'Anyway I succeeded,' he tells himself. 'Or at least I didn't fail.' Why does it feel like a letdown?" He then hears Miranda's voice saying, "the rarer action is / In virtue than in vengeance" and thinks that "she's prompting him" (246) to move on. Miranda's words come directly from the final act of *The Tempest*; Prospero says them to Ariel (75).

Felix returns to the prison for the final class period, when the men share the afterlives they've created for their characters and then celebrate at a cast party. The actors ask him to disclose the ninth prison, to which he alluded earlier in the novel. Felix says the play itself is Prospero's prison and, unless the audience "vote the play a success by clapping and cheering, Prospero will stay imprisoned on the island" (281). He points the men to the last line of the play—"As you from crimes would pardoned be, / Let your indulgence set me free" (281). Felix explains further, "the last three words in the play are 'set me free,' . . . You don't say 'set me free' unless you're not free" (282).

The novel ends with Felix's trying to cheer himself up by remembering his success: "he got his revenge" (287). He also has an epiphany: "he's been wrong about his *Tempest*, wrong for twelve years. The endgame of his obsession wasn't to bring his Miranda back to life" (291). St. John Mandel notes that, indeed, in the novel, "Miranda is trapped as surely as Ariel and Caliban" ("Brave New World"), presumably by Felix's need for her. Felix realizes that in continuing to mourn his daughter, he has been selfish by keeping Miranda "tethered to him all this time" in his imagination; he sets her free (291–92). In a final parallel to Shakespeare's play, this act frees him as well. As Howells argues, "finally, he is able to let go of his obsession with his dead Miranda, and in doing so, he prepares to give his own story a different ending" ("True Trash," 313). This ending includes a job on a cruise ship that Estelle has arranged where he will "give a couple of lectures about his wonderful theatre experiments at Fletcher Correctional" (290).

Although gender dynamics and gender relations are not major themes in this novel, Atwood's consistent interest in them is clear. There is Estelle's obvious interest in building a more intimate relationship with Felix and his careful attempts to stay in her good graces without leading her on. At the end of the novel, we learn that she plans to go on the cruise with him, leaving open the question of whether they will end up in a romantic relationship. There is the fiercely heteronormative environment of the prison, policed diligently by both the inmates and the guards. For example, when he tells the prison guards that the play choice for the year is *The Tempest*, one of them identifies it as "the one with the fairies" and "doesn't sound too pleased" (76), foreshadowing the initial negative reaction from his actors. When he tells the actors that Anne-Marie will be playing Miranda, there is some sexual innuendo. Felix warns them against any such continued behavior: "any trouble—pestering, groping, pinching, dirty talk, and so forth—and she's gone, and so are you" (89). Anne-Marie herself is fairly incredulous at the invitation to participate in the prison play; she asks unbelievingly, "you want me to go inside a prison with nothing but a lot of men criminals and do Miranda?" (98). After he explains that none of the men were willing to play a girl, she empathizes, sharing that "being the girl is the pits, trust me" (98), clearly commenting on the experiences of women in a patriarchal society. And, although his relationship with Miranda generally seems like a normal father–daughter relationship (if anything about talking to an invisible girl is normal), there is at least one moment where he falls into gender stereotyping. One day before he leaves for the prison, he thinks Miranda's been "brooding," and jokingly advises her, "You can do some embroidery" (62). After she makes her displeasure clear, he corrects his advice to suggest doing "some higher math" (62). Whether examining his relationship with Miranda or exploring Felix's experience directing his actors in prison, Atwood is clearly interested in structures of power and how they operate.

CHAPTER 4

The *MaddAddam* Trilogy
The World as We Know It Ends

Chapter 4 explores the *MaddAddam* trilogy, consisting of *Oryx and Crake* (2003, shortlisted for the Booker Prize), *The Year of the Flood* (2009), and *MaddAddam* (2013). Atwood describes this trilogy as "a series exploring another kind of 'other world'—our own planet in a future" (*In Other Worlds*, 5). Reviewer Carolyn Clay describes *Oryx and Crake* as a "barely futuristic fantasy," hinting at how entirely possible such a future might be ("Grave New World"). A review in *The Economist* agrees, noting that the entire trilogy is "set in a wholly believable dystopian future" ("Darkness and Light"). In response to readers who might question the believability of the future she's created, Atwood points out in several interviews that "many of her novel's seemingly far-fetched inventions had, in fact, already become reality" ("Atwood on the Science Behind '*Oryx and Crake*'"). As often is the case with Atwood's work, the novel is motivated by a question: "the *what if* of *Oryx and Crake* is simply: *what if we continue down the road we're already on?*" (Atwood, "Writing *Oryx and Crake*, 323, emphasis in original). She notes that "writers write about what worries them, and the world of *Oryx and Crake* is what worries me right now" (323). This novel has been optioned for development into a TV series, first in 2016 by HBO, then in 2018 by Paramount Television and, most recently, in 2021 by Hulu. Additionally, "MADDADDAM," a ballet choreographed by Wayne McGregor based on the trilogy of dystopian novels, "will finally make its world premiere as part of the National Ballet of Canada's 2022–23 season. . . . Themes of extinction and invention, hubris and humanity are spliced together with aspects of Atwood's activism and her deep connection to the Canadian landscape, past and present," the ballet said in a news release (Yeo, "Wayne McGregor-Margaret Atwood Ballet").

The trilogy contains an almost overwhelmingly dystopic future. However, there are moments of hope as well. In fact, Atwood argues for the inseparability of the utopia / dystopia combination, suggesting that "every utopia has a dystopia concealed within it. And every dystopia has got a utopia concealed within it, otherwise you wouldn't have anything to judge the 'bad' by" (Geek's Guide, "Interview"). Fredric Jameson agrees, finding that in *Oryx and Crake*, "two dystopias and a utopia were ingeniously intertwined" ("Then You Are Them"). He also argues that the "post-catastrophe situation" in *Oryx and Crake* and *The Year of the Flood* are "the preparation for the emergence of Utopia itself." Surprisingly and counterintuitively, Atwood suggests that part of the utopian landscape comes from Crake, a scientist who tries to destroy humanity in *Oryx and Crake*: "the utopian thinking, of course, is done by Crake himself, things are going to be so much better, except first we have to get rid of "those people" at a moment when "those people" are 'the human race'" (Geek's Guide, "Interview"). Bland, on the other hand, locates the utopian moments in the final two volumes where "there's this utopian vision emerging from a spiritual survivalist movement, God's Gardeners" ("It's 'Scary'").

Oryx and Crake (2003) is a tale of scientific hubris, environmental devastation, and worldwide death; Sady Doyle calls it "the bleakest of the series" ("Dystopia, for the 'Lulz'"). Robert Potts frames it as dealing "with genetic engineering in a society of increasing social division, and a misguided eugenicist's engineering of atrocity" ("Light in the Wilderness"). Slawomir Kuźnicki suggests that "the novel's reality consists of two separate realms that seem to contradict and complement each other: dehumanized science vs. human morality" (*Margaret Atwood's Dystopian Fiction*, 80), while Wisker describes it as "a tale about ecological disaster and the survival of humans in their most basic form" (*Margaret Atwood*, 152). Showalter argues that Atwood herself "also explains that the plot of *Oryx and Crake* evolved from ideas about bioengineering and human folly that had intrigued her for years" ("The Snowman Cometh").

The novel opens with a bleak scene of Snowman, whose name in the past was Jimmy, who lives by the shore with the Crakers, a genetically engineered kind of "quasi-human" (Atwood, "The Road to Ustopia"). MacPherson argues that "there is no one left but him to record the past, which he does in fits and starts, showing how his own individual past is part of a larger narrative of destruction" (78).

Jimmy is struggling to survive, stockpiling crumbs and things from "before," thus encouraging the reader to ask, "before what?" (7). As Katherine

V. Snyder points out, "we don't immediately understand what has happened to Snowman's world, or when, but as we continue to read, we apprehend that Snowman believes himself to be the sole survivor of a global pandemic that has extinguished the rest of humanity" ("'Time to Go,'" 471); since the pandemic, Jimmy has seen no evidence of any other humans. *Oryx and Crake* centers the life stories of Jimmy and Glenn (who becomes Crake, named after the rare red-headed crake which Atwood once saw in Australia), who are good friends as adolescents; as adults they are friends who are somewhat jealous and resentful of one another (Atwood, *"The Handmaid's Tale* and *Oryx and Crake,"* 515). Genetically engineered animals, formerly confined, have found their way into the wild. There are pigoons, a pig / human blend, who are dangerous and smart; there are liobams, a mix of lions and lambs; and there are Mo'Hair sheep, who were bred to grow hair for hair transplants for humans. The story is told in flashbacks and alternates between past and present, filling in the backstory at the same time as we see Jimmy experiencing his present.

Jimmy's family lives in a guarded, gated, economically prosperous community; there are several of these, referred to as Compounds and protected from the pleeblands. The pleebland cities are unsafe, with "people cruising around in those places who could forge anything and who might be anybody, not to mention the loose change—the addicts, the muggers, the paupers, the crazies" (27). In addition to the dangers of the pleebs, the global environment is collapsing: "the coastal aquifers turned salty and the northern permafrost melted and the vast tundra bubbled with methane, and the drought in the midcontinental plains regions went on and on, and the Asian steppes turned to sand dunes" (24). The world is also being impacted, negatively or positively, depending on the source, by the scientific research and business activities happening at the Compounds. Tolan notes that "the social reality of the period in which Jimmy grows up has already moved crucially beyond the limits of contemporary Western society" and that Jimmy is "unable to provide the reader with a depiction of the world in which scientific advancement and global capitalism are tempered by social and ethical responsibility" (*Margaret Atwood*, 277).

Jimmy's father is a scientist engaged in gene manipulation first for OrganIncFarms and then for NooSkins, "a subsidiary of HelthWyzer" (53). His mother, who had also worked as a scientist for OrganIncFarms, now stays home, depressed, unhappy, and prone to instigating fights with her husband. These fights generally revolve around the work in which he is engaged or the work more generally of the Compounds. In one of these arguments, Jimmy's mother refers to the work as "a moral cesspool" (56) and "sacrilegious" (57). As a young boy, Jimmy can't really understand the significance of these fights, but they serve as an indication to the reader that the corporation's work may not be above board. Periodically Jimmy visits his father at work, especially when "his mother was feeling harried" (24). One of his favorite things to do on these visits, where he always eats with his father in the Compound cafeteria, is to visit the pigoons. He's a little afraid of the adults, but "he especially liked the small pigoons" (26). Jimmy's father warns him about how dangerous they are, but Jimmy is sure they won't hurt him "because I'm their friend . . . Because I sing to them" (26). This belief appears to be a childish delusion; there is no evidence that they aren't potentially deadly. Jimmy's mother, Sharon, alternately ignores Jimmy, expresses irritation with him, or focuses on him with unsettling attention; when Jimmy is a teenager, she abandons the family. As part of her departure, she destroys his father's and her own home computer, possibly in an attempt to erase some of the data or as an expression of her continued hostility—or both. She also takes Killer, Jimmy's pet rakunk and plans to free it. Jimmy is infuriated by this: "how dare she? Killer was his!" (61).

Prior to Jimmy's mother abandoning the family, Glenn begins to attend Jimmy's school after his father has been recruited by NooSkins; the two become friends. The two boys amuse themselves by playing video games of annihilation and watching executions and pornography. Kuźnicki notes that "virtual pornography, together with cyber violence, constitute the main area of interest for teenage Jimmy and Crake" (*Margaret Atwood's Dystopian Fiction*, 92). Perhaps this foreshadows Crake's interest in death and destruction throughout his life. Here the two boys adopt their code names, selected by Crake. Jimmy's code name, which is Thickney, a "defunct Australian double-jointed bird that used to hang around in cemeteries" doesn't stick, although Crake's does (81). Crake's favorite game is Extinctathon, monitored by MaddAddam, the game's Grandmasters. It is "an interactive biofreak masterlore game" that pairs you with a challenger who will ask questions about a particular extinct species; the player is to guess the species (80). The MaddAddam Grandmasters seem to have "brains like search engines" (91); they will continue to appear throughout the trilogy.

Although the continued advances of science are celebrated by many, resistance begins to grow beyond that demonstrated by Jimmy's mother. One example is the organized resistance that mobilizes around the "gen-mod coffee wars" (178), a protest against genetically modified coffee beans, which are sold at Happicuppa franchises. The objections to the modified bean are that "it was designed so that all of its beans would ripen simultaneously, and coffee could be grown on huge plantations and harvested with machines," thus throwing small growers into poverty (179).

Jimmy and Glenn, now known by everyone as Crake, attend different colleges, reflecting the gap in their high school academic achievements and maybe their intellectual capabilities. Jimmy is a lackluster student, and it's not clear whether his mediocre academic showing is due to lack of effort or lack of ability. Crake is recruited to the prestigious Watson-Crick Institute, which focuses on science, while Jimmy is relegated to the mid-level Martha Graham Academy, which focuses on the arts. Although Jimmy recognizes the difference in the quality of these colleges, both in terms of academic reputation and the student experience, it's when Jimmy visits Crake that he can see that, "compared with Martha Graham, Watson-Crick was a palace" (199): Additionally, "the food in Crake's faculty dining hall was fantastic" (208)—real food, not the genetically modified, mass-produced food most people eat.

During Jimmy's visit to Glenn while he's in college, Glenn shares his discovery that HeathWyzer is actually making people sick so they will buy the HeathWyzer purported cures and antidotes "so they're guaranteed high profits" (211). Glenn's father had also known this, which is why, Glenn hypothesizes, his father was killed. He also discovers that MaddAddam is involved in some of the high-powered resistance to corporate hegemony and tells Jimmy, "I think they're after the machinery. They're after the whole system, they want to shut it down" (217). Glenn also appears to want to take the system down. In further conversation with Jimmy during his visit, Glenn hints at the plan taking shape in his mind, noting that if "civilization as we know it gets destroyed," it could never be rebuilt because "all of the available surface metals have already been mined" (223). Crake notes that all it would take "is the elimination of one generation" and "it's game over forever" (223). He seems untroubled by this conclusion.

After graduation Jimmy and Crake move on to jobs—Jimmy to an unsatisfying advertising job at the AnooYoo Compound and Crake at RejoovenEsense, "one of the most powerful Compounds of them all," working as a scientist (253). The CorpSeCorps has continued to visit Jimmy periodically to see if he has had heard from his mother. After he had been at AnooYoo for several years, they visit again with a video of a "routine execution" (258); his mother is one of the victims shot. Just before her murder, her blindfold is removed and his mother looks directly at the camera, saying "*goodbye. Remember Killer. I love you. Don't let me down*" (258). It is not clear what this cryptic message is supposed to mean, and Jimmy wonders "why did she have to drag Killer into it? So he'd know it was really her, that's why. So he'd believe her. But what did she mean about letting her down?" (259). This question is never answered. Does Jimmy's mother want him to refuse to work at what she sees as immoral and unethical corporations? Does she want him to join the resistance and continue her struggle? Readers do not know.

Soon, Crake recruits Jimmy to switch compounds in order to work in his unit, Paradice. Although aware of HeathWyzer's malfeasance (and presumably that of other compounds) and attracted earlier in his life to the idea of MaddAddam working against—or maybe destroying—the system, Crake remains fascinated with scientific research, particularly his own. He tells Jimmy that there are two major projects underway in which he is involved. The first is the BlyssPlussPill, designed to protect against sexually transmitted diseases, increase "libido and sexual prowess" and "prolong youth" (294). It will also, Crake shares, decrease the population level by providing permanent birth control. The Compound won't share this feature with consumers which, as Jimmy notes, means that they're "going to sterilize people without them knowing it" (294). Crake does not appear troubled by this failure to disclose a serious side effect of the medication to consumers. Jimmy's job will be the ad campaign for the pills.

The second big project is "Crake's life work"—the invention and production of the Crakers, who live inside the Paradice dome in a controlled environment (302). He has recruited (or blackmailed as we learn in *The Year of the Flood*) the MaddAddam Grandmasters to work as his "gene splicers" (298). In *MaddAddam*, they refer to themselves when they were Paradice workers as "the brain slaves" and "the captive science brainiacs" (43) and suggest that the reason Crake was "feeding us stuff from the Corps through the MaddAddam chat room" was "because he was setting us up so he could drag us into the Paradice dome to do his people-splicing for him" (334). Critics have noted the intertexual references of this scientific project to other fictional scientists. For example, Kuźnicki calls out the "obvious similarities between Crake and Doctor Frankenstein" (*Margaret Atwood's Dystopian Fiction*, 81), and Earl Ingersoll refers to Crake as "the Mad Scientist figure" ("Survival in Margaret Atwood's Novel *Oryx and Crake*," 164). Although Elaine Showalter notes that "like all mad scientists in literature, from Dr Moreau to Dr Strangelove, Crake would rather destroy than create life," that doesn't seem to be entirely true ("The Snowman Cometh"), unless one wants to argue erroneously that the Crakers are not alive. Of course, Crake has no compunction about destroying actual human life.

When Crake designs the Crakers, he wants to engineer a humanlike being without human flaws: they don't register skin color, so there's no racism and they can't create hierarchy; also "there was no territoriality," so there will be no wars over land or resources (305). They are vegetarians and "eat mostly grass and leaves and roots" (158) and are thus "engineered to live in harmony with their environment" (Ingersoll, "Survival in Margaret Atwood's Novel *Oryx and Crake*," 170). He equips them with a self-healing device; they heal themselves by purring like cats. They also purr over various injured humans in the trilogy but it is unclear whether this treatment is actually efficacious for the humans (156). They have "UV-resistant skin, a built-in insect repellent . . . [and] immunity from microbes," so they are not in danger from environmental contamination (304). The women come into heat every three years, a state which is signaled by their abdomens turning blue; the men then respond to this physiologically as their penises turn blue as well. The women select four men from the group to mate with and they "go at it until the woman becomes pregnant" (165). Crake has even "equipped these women with ultra-strong vulvas—extra skin layers, extra muscles—so they can sustain these marathons" (165). Asserting that "human sexuality produces much misery and violence as the result of unfulfilled desire" (Ingersoll, "Survival in Margaret Atwood's Novel *Oryx and Crake*," 166), Crake has eliminated love and other such complications; the purpose of sex is simply to procreate. The Crakers will "drop dead at age thirty" without sickness or old age (303). It's a highly ambitious project and seems a bit like playing God. Crake finds the Crakers, and other versions that might be created later, a "superior method" for reproduction (304). Ursula Le Guin disagrees, bitingly asking "Who wants to be replaced by people who turn blue when they want sex" ("The Year of the Flood"). Tolan is also skeptical, noting that for the Crakers, "gender remains, but deprived of its cultural expression, it is reduced to biological function" (*Margaret Atwood*, 295), implying that this is a very limited way to be in the world or perhaps to be in relation to others.

Jimmy learns that Oryx[1] has been hired by Crake to serve as the Crakers' teacher. Jimmy and Crake initially discover Oryx as teenagers on one of the child porn sites they favor. Jimmy is immediately captivated by her, feeling that when she looks into the camera, she is seeing "right into the eyes of the viewer—right into Jimmy's eyes, into the secret person inside him" (91); feeling seen in this way also makes him uneasy about their consumption of porn, or at least child porn; "for the first time he'd felt that what they'd been doing was wrong" (91). Crake encounters her again through Student Services at his college; one of the services provided by the college is to arrange for sex workers for the students. No such service exists for Jimmy at the Martha Graham Academy. Crake later "made private arrangements" for Oryx to work for him (310). In addition to socializing and teaching the Crackers, Oryx is part of the BlyssPluss project and makes sales trips to distribute pills in other cities and countries. While at RejoovenEsense, she is Crake's lover and also becomes Jimmy's lover, saying that she didn't want Jimmy to be unhappy because of her (312). Karen Stein notes that the men "utilize her for sexual purposes and as a medium of exchange between them" ("Surviving the Waterless Flood," 321), suggesting that their relationship—at least in part—is "based on status and competition" (328). In fact, Jimmy often wonders whether Crake knows about his sexual relationship with Oryx and presumes that he does.

Oryx has haunted Jimmy throughout his life; after they meet and become lovers, he probes for information about her past. She is evasive; Tolan argues that she is "an enigma" and "one of Atwood's most ambiguous characters to date" (*Margaret Atwood*, 287, 286). Oryx resists answering Jimmy's questions and refuses to narrate or reflect on her experiences in the ways he expects. He notes that "she was never very forthcoming in the best of times" (114), responding to his questions with answers like "I don't know. I've forgotten" (114) and "you want me to make something up" (92). He is eventually able to "piece her together from the slivers of her he'd gathered and hoarded so carefully" (114). His story of Oryx is told in chronological order, unlike most of the novel. Although Jimmy is avidly trying to discover Oryx's true history, he comes to see that there are multiple ways to understand Oryx's life. He thinks, "there was Crake's story about her, and Jimmy's story about her as well, a more romantic version; and then there was her own story about herself" (114), to which she denies him access. After she is dead, Snowman feels her spirit with him at times, hearing her voice inside his head and occasionally responding to her.

In retrospect, Jimmy identifies more indicators from Crake about his plans for the future; "there were signs and I missed them" (320). Crake and Oryx each ask him to take over the Paradice Project and tend to the Crakers if anything should happen to them, leading us to wonder why they thought something might happen to them. However, shortly after these conversations, the plague, "a rogue hemorrhagic," spreads worldwide (325), causing mass death and panic. Oryx phones to tell Jimmy she's discovered the source was in the BlyssPluss pills she'd been marketing. She's crying. Her tears demonstrate a depth of emotion we have not seen from Oryx, and it is "so unusual Jimmy was rattled by it" (325). Shortly afterwards, Crake comes to Paradice with an unconscious Oryx in his arms to tell Jimmy that both Jimmy and Crake are protected from the plague's impacts because the antibody was "in the plebe vaccine" that they protectively administered to themselves before they went slumming in the pleeblands (328). Crake has "anticipated this event and took precautions" (328); he clearly planned it. Oddly enough, it doesn't seem that Crake has given Oryx the vaccine. Crake kills Oryx and Jimmy responds by killing him.

There is a sense that Crake *wants* Jimmy to kill him; he says to Jimmy "I'm counting on you" before he kills Oryx (329). This might indicate that Crake is aware of Jimmy's deep feelings for Oryx and assumes that if he kills Oryx, Jimmy will respond accordingly out of revenge. We can only speculate about Crake's motives. Was he always planning this end to his life? Did he suddenly develop a moral compass and regret his actions? Was Oryx vulnerable to the plague, not having been vaccinated and was he trying, in some perverse way, to protect her? Why didn't he give her the vaccine? Although nowhere in the novel are we told of Crake's feelings for Oryx, in opposition to what we know of Jimmy's, he must have some or he wouldn't have asked her to come and work with him. And why did he need Jimmy to kill him instead of committing suicide? All of these questions remain unanswered.

Jimmy stays locked inside Paradice while the world continues to collapse. Eventually he realizes that the Crakers will run out of the vegetation on which they feed so he decides to take them to the shore to live, "where there will be more to eat" (349). He renames himself Snowman, feeling that "he no longer wanted to be Jimmy" (348). The Crakers are insatiably curious about Crake and Oryx, who made them, or so Jimmy has told them. In response, Snowman invents the creation stories of the Children of Oryx and the Children of Crake. Snowman finds that the Crakers value consistency and "like repetition" (309) in the tales; "now they're demanding dogma: he would deviate from orthodoxy at his peril" (104). Snowman also pretends to receive messages from Crake to instruct the Crakers about things Jimmy needs; for example, he tells them that Crake wants the Crakers to bring Snowman a fish every week. Soon, Snowman realizes that "he's slowly starving to death" (147), as he exhausts his supply of foodstuffs and provisions he's been able to scrounge nearby; he must venture further afield even though he doesn't know what dangers he might encounter.

Jimmy heads to the Paradise Dome to restock because he knows there are supplies remaining there; he injures his foot in the journey. It's a difficult journey, but Jimmy makes it to the compound, gleaning from houses, some populated by dead bodies, on his way to the Dome. At one point, Jimmy encounters a band of pigoons and we see why they are so dangerous to humans. They first move out of sight, but Jimmy is suspicious as they "are clever enough to fake a retreat, then lurk around the next corner" (235). They are "a brainy and omnivorous animal" with "human neocortex tissue growing in their crafty, wicked heads" (235). Emerging from the guardhouse in which he had taken refuge, the pigoons appear again. There are two groups of them, and their intent seems clear. It's "as if they've known for some time that he was in the gatehouse and have been waiting for him to come out, far enough out so they can surround him" (267). He barricades himself back in the guardhouse but can hear them crashing into the door to get in. Jimmy is desperately thinking of how to escape when he sees closed doors on the other side of the room, one of which opens, leading him to some stairs which lead to a watchtower. This is an unexpected benefit because the pigoons "have short legs and fat stomachs" (269) and will be unable to climb the stairs. Jimmy realizes that he dropped the garbage bag full of the things he's collected to take back to the shore, but he is unable to retrieve it because the pigoons are lying in wait.

Jimmy finds a treasure trove of food and equipment in the guardhouse. There is also a wind-up radio. This is our first indication that at least one other human has survived as Jimmy hears a man asking "Is anyone reading me? Anyone out there? Do you read me? Over?" (273). There is no response to Jimmy's reply but he suddenly realizes that he doesn't know "who's at the other end" (274); the man might not be friendly. After a pause to rest and resupply, Jimmy manages to get out of the watchtower through an air vent, which deposits him on the compound's rampart, "meant for observation but useful too for the emplacement of last-ditch weaponry" (279). Jimmy plans to get to the Paradice dome, restock, and then sneak out of the compound before the pigoons can find him. As he walks on the rampart, he sees a second sign of humanity, smoke from a fire. Jimmy makes it to the dome, encountering Crake and Oryx's dead bodies. He finds the supplies and also treats his injured foot, which is clearly infected.

When he returns to the shore with his bounty, he finds the Crakers chanting some words while sitting around "a scarecrowlike effigy" (360) they have created. It sounds to him like they are saying Amen although it turns out they are chanting "Snowman." Jimmy is surprised to observe them involved in what seems to be some kind of religious or spiritual ritual since Crake had designed them to be "free of all contamination of that kind" (360). However, at least this aspect of their design appears to be evolving. When the Crakers discover that he is back, they tell him that "we knew we could call you, and you would hear us and come back" (360). Furthermore, they explain the effigy, saying that "we made a picture of you, to help us send out our voices to you" (361). This is the first time we sense some kind of telepathic connection, at least between the Crakers and Jimmy, although it is not at all clear that this chanting or calling from the Crakers actually contributes anything to his safe return. Jimmy recalls Crake saying that "*as soon as they start doing art, we're in trouble*" (361, emphasis in original). Crake thought that "symbolic thinking of any kind" would be a problem (361).

Jimmy learns from the Crakers that other humans had been to their encampment at the shore, a few men and a woman. At least one of them is armed; Jimmy himself has a spraygun he retrieved from the Dome. He wonders if the humans "have been frightened off . . . Maybe they're ill and dying. Or maybe not" (366). After a night's rest, he stealthily goes in search of them. The novel concludes as he comes upon them and tries to decide how and whether to approach them. Should he try to scare them off? Should he preemptively shoot them as a measure of protection? There is no way for us to anticipate what his decision will be or what the response of the other human beings will be. Tolan describes this lack of closure as Atwood's decision to end the novel on "a note of ambiguous indecision" (*Margaret Atwood*, 296).

Oryx and Crake was short-listed for the 2003 Man Booker Prize for Fiction and for the 2004 Orange Prize for Fiction, although critical reception to the novel was mixed. Nick Turner notes that some claim it is "not her strongest work" ("Margaret Atwood"). Sven Birkets argues that it negatively "elevates scenario over sensibility" ("Present at the Re-Creation"). In contrast, *Kirkus Reviews* calls the novel "ingenious and disturbing" and argues that "Atwood has surpassed herself" ("Oryx and Crake").

As with several of Atwood's other novels, *Oryx and Crake* is primarily a nonlinear narrative. Always told through Jimmy's perspective, it alternates between his current reality and the actions and experiences that led to that reality. It also offers an opportunity to reflect on the nature of storytelling. We hear the stories Jimmy tells the Crakers that explain what's going on with their history as well as the stories he tells himself, both as he experiences his life in the moment and as he reflects on his history and experiences. Tolan notes that this choice of the gender of protagonist(t)s is unusual; the novel is Atwood's "first to employ a primary male protagonist" (it precedes *Hag-Seed*), and she reads this choice as signifying "the loss of the female voice" (*Margaret Atwood*, 273). In part, Tolan's conclusion might stem from our lack of access to Oryx's perspective. However, while Oryx's voice and perspectives are less prominent than either Jimmy's or Crake's, despite Jimmy's fixation with her, she is very much a presence in the novel. In fact, some of the ways Oryx is positioned in the novel might be *because* of Jimmy's obsession with her. For much of the novel she is on his mind, in his head, or in his bed.

The subject matter of *Oryx and Crake* also allows Atwood to look critically at scientific advances in bioengineering and genome manipulation, areas that are clearly a concern for her. Ingersoll suggests the novel is "a believable extrapolation of contemporary nightmares" ("Survival in Margaret Atwood's Novel *Oryx and Crake*," 164). In this way, the novel serves as a cautionary tale just as *The Handmaid's Tale* does. In fact, as Ingersoll notes, Atwood herself encourages "readers to connect these two examples of what she likes to term 'speculative fiction'" (162).

Oryx and Crake was followed by *The Year of the Flood* (2009), which Atwood refers to as "a sibling book" ("Margaret Atwood: The Road to Ustopia"). The two novels take place in the same time period, with some of the same characters and intersecting stories. As Atwood notes, "they are more like chapters of the same book" ("Margaret Atwood: The Road to Ustopia"). Stein argues that both novels "investigate the dangers of a flawed social order that values profits above people and that accords the most prestigious caste unlimited power to use technology to change the world" ("Surviving the Waterless Flood," 320). Kuźnicki comments that "the plot of *The Year of the Flood* centres on the same period of time and the same events depicted in *Oryx and Crake* but does so by employing a completely different perspective" (*Margaret Atwood's Dystopian Fiction*, 121). J. Brooks Bouson describes the novel as providing "a feminist re-telling and re-visioning of *Oryx and Crake*'s male-centered apocalyptic end-of-the-world story" ("On Margaret Atwood," 21).

As Bouson notes, *The Year of the Flood* is told primarily by two women, Toby and Ren, as well as by God's Gardeners, a small eco-survivalist group organized by Adam One, who is thought to be Zeb's stepbrother. Interspersed with these narratives are Adam's sermons and the Gardeners' hymns, which commemorate festival days.[2] The festival days are in honor of the saints the Gardeners have selected, choosing "people who have been notable for their egalitarian and environmental values" (Stein, "Surviving the Waterless Flood," 332). Felicia R. Lee describes the Gardeners as "an ascetic cult whose religion inculcates reverence for the environment and animals and a respect for science that rests on the belief that the creation story cannot be taken literally" ("Back to the Scary Future"). Le Guin calls the group "a vividly memorable invention" ("The Year of the Flood"), while John Barber suggests that their role is "to serve as a naively optimistic antidote to an otherwise horrific scenario" ("Atwood: 'Have I Ever Eaten Maggots?'"). The Gardeners also seem to be practicing anti-capitalists. They barter and salvage, making as much of what they need as they can. They can't entirely disconnect from the capitalist system; they do sell vegetables and homemade vinegar at the Tree of Life Market Natural Materials Exchange, where other vendors sell products as well—primarily to the "affluents"' from the Compounds (141).

The Gardeners also have reframed depression, characterizing it as a "Fallow state," which is described as "resting, retreating into themselves to gain Spiritual insight, gathering their energy for the moment when they would burst out again like buds in spring. They only appeared to be doing nothing" (80). Throughout the novel, we see a few people moving in and out of a Fallow phase: Bernice's mother Veena is one. She's spending her Fallow experience at home, but there is also a Fallows Hut for people in a Fallow phase. It is notable that there is a separate space for those who are Fallow, indicating that the experience is integrated into the community and not stigmatized. Although Fallowness does not play a significant role in the novel's narrative, taking the time for rest and rejuvenation can certainly be read as a protest against capitalism, which requires people to be ceaselessly productive. Pilar also spends time in the

Fallows hut, but she appears to be ill rather than Fallow; she is conscious and interacts with others.

As with *Oryx and Crake,* this novel also uses a nonlinear timeline with flashbacks and memories. It begins after the plague—caused by Crake, as we know—that destroyed most of humanity. God's Gardeners refer to it as the "Waterless Flood," drawing a parallel to the flood Noah escaped in his ark (7). The narrative begins with Toby sheltering safely inside the locked AnooYoo Spa; she wonders, as did Snowman, whether she's the only person left on the planet. Ren is safely in protective quarantine at Scales and Tales, one of the SeksMarts in the pleeblands offering erotic performances and sex; her prophylactic Biofilm Bodyglove (6) was ripped while providing services to a customer. Thus, out of an abundance of caution, she is placed in quarantine until her test results are back. Scales, Ren says, "had a reputation to keep up: we were known as the cleanest dirty girls in town" (7). They both have access to food, although Toby is cultivating a garden as "her supplies in the [Spa's] storeroom are getting low" (15). Following the Gardeners' practices, she had been stockpiling food prior to the Flood.

As a college student, Toby was orphaned when her mother becomes ill and dies, despite the preventative HelthWyzer Hi-Potency VitalVite supplements she took daily; her father subsequently commits suicide. Toby disappears into the pleeblands so that the CorpSeCorps don't "come after her for her father's debts" (31). Barely existing, she finally gets a job at the fast-food chain Secret-Burgers, where she makes dismally low wages but earns two meals a day. The meat at SecretBurgers is highly suspect, because "no one knew what sort of animal protein was actually in them" (33). Besides the meager pay, there is another significant drawback to working at SecretBurgers. The violent and intimidating manager, Blanco, uses the female workers for sex, whether they are willing or not. Eventually he chooses Toby. She is desperate to resist him but feels she has no other options. She thinks, "where else could she go? She lived from pay to pay. She had no money" (36). Laurie Vickroy notes that the novel reflects Atwood's "long-term interest in the power politics of gender relations . . . [and] offers gruesome descriptions of male violence against women in an environmentally devastated and posthuman future" ("Sexual Trauma, Ethics, and the Reader," 274). One of the most graphic examples of this in the novel is the violence doled out by Blanco, primarily although not exclusively to women. Toby becomes increasingly desperate; "despair was taking her over: she could see where this was going, and it looked like a dark tunnel. She'd be used up soon" (39).

When a group of God's Gardeners stops at the restaurant to proselytize against meat-eating, a scuffle ensues. Blanco is injured and Toby escapes with the encouragement of the members of the Gardeners. Toby discovers that the Gardeners do really garden; they have gardens planted on roofs. The main Gardener location also has a beehive. There is a significant focus on sustainability and self-sufficiency. Stein suggests that "the culture of God's Gardeners, however imperfect and off-kilter it may be, points toward an alternative, ecofeminist, value system of commonality, frugality, and respect for the environment and living things" ("Surviving the Waterless Flood," 330).

The Adams and Eves are the most respected of the Gardeners and serve as a loose governance structure, although there is purportedly no hierarchy. Toby is asked to use her knowledge of Holistic Healing to enrich the community. So, in addition to the other domestic work she takes on, Toby prepares "herbal lotions and creams" (46) and also offers classes to other Gardeners. Toby gains additional expertise and knowledge from Pilar, who is an herbalist, healer, and beekeeper. Pilar believes Toby's mother was killed by HelthWyzer and that the corporation was using customers as guinea pigs to test products, equally as nefarious as the corporate practices Crake disclosed in *Oryx and Crake*. After Pilar's death, Toby takes Pilar's place as healer and beekeeper; she also is chosen to become an Eve.

Toby resists Adam One's invitation to become an Eve, telling him, "it would be hypocritical" because "'I'm not sure I believe in all of it.' An understatement: she believed in very little" (168). Adam is not perturbed by this confession, pointing out that "in some religions, faith precedes action. . . In ours, action precedes faith" (168).

As she assumes these new duties, Toby learns more about how the Adams and Eves function. At their periodic meetings, "they sat around a table like any other conclave and hammered out their positions" (189). She finds that, contrary to her belief that they were a small fringe group, "they were growing in influence . . . they had branches in different pleebs, and even in other cities" (189). The purpose of these branches is initially unclear to Toby, other than improving the odds of the community to survive when the Waterless Flood is unleashed. However, she soon learns that their goals are bigger than mere survival: "they also had cells of hidden Exfernal sympathizers embedded at every level, even within the Corporations themselves" (189), providing information about what the corporations, "their enemies, are doing" (190). It is not clear whether the Gardeners' interest in these corporate activities is limited to just gaining the information to protect themselves, or whether there are plans to impact the corporations' activities in some way, such as sabotage or attempted destruction.

Ren and Toby meet when Ren's mother, Lucerne, and her Gardener boyfriend, Zeb, take her as a child to live with the Gardeners. Ren lived at the

HelthWyzer compound with her mother and father until Lucerne decides to leave Ren's father to come to the Gardeners with Zeb, one of the Adams. Ren is unhappy at being forced to leave the compound; she "didn't like it [at the Gardeners] at all" (59). However, she becomes more content once Amanda, another young girl, joins the Gardeners. They become close friends when she encounters Amanda living on the streets and brings her home. Ren feels that "we're each other's family," in contrast to the distance she feels between Lucerne and herself (56). Lucerne and Zeb fight constantly, so the girls become support systems for one another. Amanda, who in *Oryx and Crake* was briefly Jimmy's college girlfriend, becomes an artist who creates Bioart installations—she writes a word using animal bones, covers it with syrup to attract insects, and then records the process of decomposition. Ren describes Amanda's artistic inspiration: she "liked to watch things move and grow and then disappear" (56).

After a particularly bad fight between Zeb and Lucerne, Lucerne decides to leave him, taking Ren back to HelthWyzer and her husband; Ren is distraught at the thought of leaving Amanda behind. In order to explain their absence, Lucerne concocts a story that they were "forcibly abducted" (207) by a cult and that Ren has "been traumatized by being stuck in among the warped, brainwashing cult folk" (213). Lucerne doesn't specify who or what the cult is. She does explain that the motivation for their abduction is that one of the male members of the cult was "obsessed with her and wanted her for his personal sex slave and had taken away her shoes to keep her captive" (210). She claims she had to obey him or Ren's life "would have been in danger" (211). Ren is sent to the Compound high school where characters from *Oryx and Crake* begin to appear. She and Jimmy become friends and then lovers. They break up when she finds him cheating on her, and she becomes friends with Glenn (later to become Crake). They had met briefly during her time at the Gardeners, when Glenn came to see Pilar who he knew from her time at HelthWyzer. Ren finds it comforting to hang out with Glenn because "Glenn was the only person at HelthWyzer I could talk to about the Gardeners, and it was the same for him" (228). When Ren eventually goes away to college, she enrolls at the Martha Graham Academy. Although her time at college overlaps with Jimmy's time at Martha Graham, they don't reconnect in any meaningful way.

While she's away at college, Ren's father is kidnapped by a rival compound. In an attempt to blackmail HelthWyzer, the kidnappers send them a video of her father "confessing that HelthWyzer had been sticking a slow-acting but incurable gene-spliced disease germ inside their supplements so they could make a lot of money on treatments" (293), thus confirming Pilar's earlier suspicion about Toby's mother's death as well as Crake's claims to Jimmy in *Oryx and Crake* about HelthWyzer's activities. The decision-makers at HelthWyzer aren't concerned with the consequences of their refusal to meet the kidnappers' demands, feeling that "they could squelch it at [the] source, since the media Corps controlled what was news and what wasn't" (293). Ren's father is abandoned and left with the kidnappers, presumably to be killed.

In addition to their control of the media, the CorpSeCorps maintains order in the compounds and the pleeblands. One mechanism of control is the PainBall games. Condemned criminals have the option to be killed or to compete on teams in the Painball Arena, with paint guns loaded with paint that corroded skin if it touched it. The contests are televised, although there isn't much to see "because the Painballers were understandably stealthy" (98); the Painballers on the winning teams are eventually released "when their time is up" (98). Former Painball competitors are extraordinarily violent and dangerous. Presumably this is because they find no behaviors unacceptable and are willing to violate all social norms and conventions.

Toby takes some comfort in being told that Blanco has been put in Painball, but she continues to worry about his eventual return and the retribution she's sure he'll exact when he gets out; her worry is intensified when Zeb tells her he's been released. Zeb sets out with a couple of the Gardener boys to "do a snoop" (251) and see if they can learn more in an effort to reassure her; they end up in a scuffle with Blanco who, realizing they are part of the Gardeners, shortly thereafter comes for revenge with two of his henchmen. The Gardeners fight them off successfully, but Blanco recognizes Toby. When he moves to attack her, she sets loose the bees, who attack him. He flees. The Adams and Eves, including Toby, realize that she endangers them all if she stays, so a decision is made to relocate her. Zeb assists with smuggling her to safety and arranges for her to have her identity and appearance changed.

After Toby recovers from the cosmetic procedures, she is given a job as manager at the AnooYoo Spa. Because Lucerne is a regular customer, Toby develops strategies to avoid her, fearing that despite her changed appearance, she might be recognized. Zeb visits, undercover as a groundsman, to update her on the latest news and to give her a way to contact the Gardeners—via the Extinctathon site monitored by MaddAddam. One day on the site, she finds a message from Zeb that "the Garden is destroyed" (271). She can't learn anything more, although the reader soon discovers that at least some of the Gardeners are safe. Adam One attributes the attacks to the fact that the Gardeners "were becoming too powerful for their [the corporations] liking" and that the Gardeners "threatened their profit margins" (275). It's unclear if this really is the motivation behind the attack or whether it is a response to the infiltration and spying of the Gardeners and their cells.

At a hiring fair at Martha Graham, Toby—as Tobiatha, the name she adopted after her appearance change—makes a job offer to Ren (295); Ren has also gotten an offer from Scales and Tails to be a dancer. She accepts the job at AnooYoo Spa and learns that Tobiatha is really Toby from the Gardeners. As with Toby, Ren also needs to avoid Lucerne when she comes to the spa but after one encounter in the hall with Lucerne, Ren feels that even though she resents her mother, "it was a very bad feeling to know that she didn't want to see me or talk to me" (301). After encountering Lucerne and after learning that Amanda is now Jimmy's girlfriend, Ren decides to leave AnooYoo to work at Scales; she feels she needs "to be on my own . . . to be someone else entirely" (301).

Because Toby lives on the premises at AnooYoo, she is able to barricade herself inside when the Waterless Flood comes. Although at times she is lonely for human interaction, at least she is safe. One day she sees three pigoons sniffing around the garden she is cultivating for extra supplies. When they start to dig under the fence, Toby frightens them off. She notes that "amazingly they seem to understand her," but another explanation comes to her quickly: "they must've seen a weapon before" and thus recognize what a danger her rifle could be to them (18). As the animals are fleeing, Toby realizes that "they'll be back. They'll dig under at night and root up her garden in no time flat, and that will be the end of her long-term food supply" (18). She shoots at them and successfully kills the boar. Although "she'd taken the Vegivows when she joined the Gardeners," she does not feel sorry at the death of the pigoon. However, despite her waning food stores, she also doesn't butcher it, continuing to feel like "animal protein should be the last resort" (19). Although earlier Toby expressed a lack of faith in the Gardeners' beliefs, she seems to have absorbed much of it; their practices continue to inform her actions. Toby wakes one morning to see that "the pigs have been back" (319) and her garden is destroyed. She observes that it "was less like a feeding frenzy than a deliberate act of revenge" (320) and notices that the pigs are waiting and watching her "as if they want to witness her dismay" (320). This comment seems to ascribe human emotions to the pigoons, even though they are animals.

Later Toby recognizes that she has to have more food and in particular "animal protein" (325). She realizes that there must be maggots on the rotting boar in the meadow and, however distasteful, that is her only option. She tries to think of them as "land shrimp," as Zeb's voice in her head advises. When she arrives at the carcass, she finds that "there are fronds scattered about on top of the boar's carcass and beside it. Fern fronds. Such ferns don't grow in the meadow." There are also "rose petals, from the roses by the driveway" (328). She remembers reading that elephants do something similar for dead ones, but she finds it unsettling: "could the pigs have been having a funeral? Could they be bringing memorial bouquets? She finds this idea truly frightening" (328). The pigoons seem to be reacting to what we would think of as human emotions: grief and sorrow in the face of loss.

The Scales manager, Mordis, thinks Ren is an excellent performer, and she finds that she enjoys the trapeze dancing, even if she "didn't like the other parts of the job that much" (303); presumably this is the sex work. Just as there is a hierarchy between the Compounds and the pleeblands, there are hierarchies at work in the club. The talent, which includes Ren, is privileged. They get "good food, a doctor if you needed one, and the tips were great, because the men from the top Corps came" to Scales (7). Talent is "a valuable asset," according to Mordis (7). There are differences among the clients too. In addition to the bigwigs from the Compounds, Painballers patronize Scales. Extra security is needed then; Ren notes that "there were always two or three CorpSeCorps guys minding the Painball vets—they could go berserk and cause a lot of damage" (129). Talent is "never allowed to be alone with them" (130) because they "are skilled artists and any damage to us would be pricey" (130). Other sex workers are brought in to service the Painballers, "the temporaries—smuggled Eurotrash or Tex-Mexicans or Asian Fusion and Redfish minors scooped off the streets" (130).

Crake, whom Ren knew as Glenn, now appears frequently at Scales with "the Mr. Bigs and his funders" of the Paradice Project; in addition to using the Scalies to treat his guests to sex, he also rents them "for some very strange things." For example, "once he wanted us to purr like cats so he could measure our vocal cords. Another time he wanted us to sing like birds so he could record us" (305). Crake is clearly doing research to assist in his design and perfecting of the Crakers, although the women at Scales have no idea of the purpose of these activities.

After the Waterless Flood caused by Crake's BlyssPluss pills, Amanda is eventually able to get Ren out of the quarantine lockup, where she has almost run out of food. They stay at Scales for several days, eating the food from the high-end suites, doing their nails, trying on the costumes, and generally entertaining themselves. One day they are surprised by a visit from Shackie, Croze, and Oates, other kids who had been raised at the Gardeners at the same time Ren and Amanda were there. They had been sent to Painball as punishment for working with MaddAddam's underground gene-splicers on bioform resistance; their isolation in the Painball Area has protected them from the plague. The reunion is interrupted when men from the Gold Painball team, including Blanco, come into Scales. Ren and her friends flee the club but know that "they'll come after us" (337); the men will be able to tell there had been people at Scales. Although they try to be careful and take steps to be less visible,

Blanco and his friends do find and capture them. Oates is killed but Croze and Shackie are able to flee. The girls are kept prisoner and raped repeatedly, more evidence of male violence.

Toby actually sees the Painballers and the women as they travel past the Spa, presumably to the shore as that is where they end up in *Oryx and Crake*. At first, Toby thinks she is hallucinating because one of the men is leading "a bird with blue-green iridescent plumes like a peagret. But this bird has the head of a woman' (350). Although Toby doesn't know it, this is Ren, still wearing the costume she had on when she and Amanda were dancing at Scales. The men notice Toby on the rooftop. She sees that they are armed with at least a knife and a spraygun and also that the bird woman is being controlled with a rope around her neck. Toby shoots at the men and wounds one but misses the others. She knows that they'll come back because "they know I'm in here, they'll guess I must have food in order to have stayed alive this long. Also, I shot one of them: they'll want revenge" (352).

During the fracas, Ren somehow escapes and circles back to the AnooYoo Spa. In part it is the closest building, but she has also spent time at the Spa and knows the terrain. She also might think that there is some possibility Toby will still be alive and taking shelter at the Spa. Ren is desperate, and the Spa is the best choice she has; even if she can't get help there, it's better than the Painballers. This is another moment when Toby's healing skills and knowledge are useful. Ren has clearly been beaten and raped, but she is also "burning with fever" and has a "festering leg wound" (355, 356). Toby nurses her back to health.

Throughout the novel, Toby is rational and strategic, but never cold, while Ren seems to operate based on loyalty and emotion. However, when Ren insists they have to try to rescue Amanda, Toby agrees—in part to humor Ren as she continues to recover, but also because "they have to move somewhere else anyway: the food supply's shrinking fast" (362). They provision themselves and set out for the shore. Blanco has remained a threatening and dangerous presence throughout most of the novel, particularly, but not only, for Toby. When Toby and Ren encounter him during their journey, fatally injured and abandoned by his comrades, Toby euthanizes him with no regret.

In a chance encounter with Croze the next day, they learn that there are other humans who survived. Croze, some of MaddAddam, and some of the Gardeners are sheltering and rebuilding in the cobb house in the park. It's a subsistence life at the moment, as life was with the Gardeners before the Garden was destroyed, although they currently have much less than the Gardeners did and have adopted this lifestyle not because of theology but out of necessity. They're herding Mo'Hairs; there is a cookhouse; they've constructed some "violet porta-biolets"; and they're working on rebuilding some solar power (389). And they're beginning to plant a garden. The group has seen the Crakers and Jimmy by the shore, although they haven't approached them. Blanco's friends passed by their encampment with Amanda. The Painballers wanted to trade Amanda "for spraygun cells and Mo'Hair meat" (389), but the group refused. In addition, they continue to search for Adam One and the other Gardeners who disappeared after the Garden was ruined.

Although Zeb tries to dissuade Toby and Ren from leaving the group so that they can search for Amanda, or at least to postpone their trip until he and others return from another search mission and can accompany them, Ren insists on resuming her attempt to rescue Amanda. Toby agrees to go with her; Ren says Toby argues that "she can't let me wander off into the woods by myself: it would be like murder" (399). They locate the Painballers and Amanda and encounter Jimmy at the shore. The Painballers have one spraygun, as does Jimmy; Toby is armed with a rifle. In the ensuing struggle, the Painballers are knocked unconscious, subdued, disarmed, and tied to trees. Amanda is liberated.

Readers see again how much Toby has absorbed the Gardeners' creed. When she realizes it's a festival day, Saint Julian and All Souls, she makes soup out of supplies she's brought along and the food the Painballers still had. Toby insists on sharing the soup with the Painballers, despite Amanda's objections, feeling that it would be wrong to show cruelty on a Feast Day; the Gardeners' practices still influence her. The novel ends with the sound of the Crakers singing and coming toward the group.

Kuźnicki notes that "similarly to *Oryx and Crake*, in *The Year of the Flood*, Atwood does not express much optimism for humankind" (*Margaret Atwood's Dystopian Fiction*, 132). In contrast, the final volume, *MaddAddam*, moves from explaining "'How did we get here?' to 'Where do we go now?'" and focuses on survival strategies and the potential for coexistence with one another and with nonhuman beings (Dutkiewicz, "MaddAddam"). Shelley Boyd describes the shift as one where the humans and Crakers "form their own makeshift community of sustenance and care" ("Utopian Breakfasts," 161). Doyle suggests that "the question of *MaddAddam* is not whether humanity should survive, but how" ("Dystopia, for the 'Lulz'"). Atwood begins with brief summaries of the first two volumes, followed by a new version of the Crake creation story, which has been updated to include the discovery of the Painballers and Amanda on the beach. The first full chapter of the novel includes the Craker men enacting their fertility ritual with Amanda, because they "smell the blue" (12); despite her protests, they rape her. They also free the prisoners, against Toby's and other's wishes, arguing that "this rope is hurting these ones. We must take it away" (12). The Painballers flee at once with their spraygun. Toby realizes they must all leave the beach and return to the cobb house to be safe, or at least safer. In addition to worrying about the Painballers returning, there are animal predators about which to be concerned. The Crakers decide to come along; two of them carry Jimmy, who was injured in his earlier journey to Paradice and, now ill, is delusional. Because Ren and Toby refer to Jimmy by his actual name, the Crakers begin to refer to him as Snowman-the-Jimmy.

In *MaddAddam*, the Crakers are infrequently referred to by name. Rather, the humans refer to them as "Craker men" (15) and "Craker women" (21). Or sometimes they are referred to by their color, as in "the gold-coloured man" (99) or the "ivory woman" (100). When they refer to Toby by name, she wonders "what are their own names, and is it polite to ask?" (26). When Toby asks one of the children his name, he tells her it is Blackbeard, which she finds a little unusual, since Blackbeard was a "notorious murdering pirate" (92). But now that she has learned some of their names (such as "Abraham Lincoln" and "Empress Josephine," 138), she thinks that "a lot of the Crakers have odd names" (92). Crake named them. She decides that "why shouldn't their names be odd, to go with their general oddity" (92).

Jimmy is conscious when they arrive at the cobb house enclave. However, the next morning, he seems to be in some kind of coma. He doesn't wake up. The Crakers have moved him outside as "he did not like it in that dark place," referring to the cobb house (37). As in *Oryx and Crake*, the Crakers seem to have some kind of telepathic connection with Jimmy, as they tell Toby that Jimmy "is travelling to here. He is running, sometimes fast and sometimes slow. Sometimes walking, because he is tired" (37). They claim that "when he gets to here, he will wake up" (37). Later they share that "now he has stopped . . . He has climbed into a tree" (99). They can also tell what he is feeling because they know that "he is afraid of what is in this world. He is afraid of the bad men, he is afraid of the Pig Ones. He doesn't want to be awake" (100). One morning they advise her that "he is walking very quickly, inside his head. Soon he will be here" (138). When he awakens, he does not seem to be in his right mind, raving about pigoons eating him and "brain spaghetti" (147). Toby is not especially concerned, remembering that "it's not uncommon for someone waking from a coma to hallucinate" (147). The Crakers, however, are concerned and move immediately to purr over Jimmy; in their view, "in his head there is something tangled" (147).

It is when Jimmy wakes up that the Crakers's lack of ability to understand anything beyond the literal becomes particularly humorous. When Jimmy is raving, he says "Oh fuck" (146). The Crakers call Toby "Oh Toby" (146) because they think that the "Oh" signifies "a term of address" (146). So, they think Fuck is a person, asking "who is this *Fuck*? . . . Why is he talking to this Fuck? That is not the name of anyone here" (146, emphasis in original). Toby explains it by saying that Fuck is with Crake and Oryx, whom the Crakers think are in the sky. They "would like to hear the story of Fuck" (147) and have decided that "we will sing to this Fuck" (148). Fuck will reappear, metaphorically speaking, at other points in the novel as well.

Toby and the group continue to be concerned about the Painballers. The men were short on ammunition when they first visited the enclave, and "they know the MaddAddam cobb house will have some. Sooner or later, they'll be tempted to attack at the weakest link: they'll grab a Craker child and offer to swap, as they tried to swap Amanda earlier" (27). As the search party begins to recover from their ordeal, the Crakers decide that Toby must take over the evening story ritual. She protests, noting that "I don't know the stories of Crake!" but they insist, arguing that "you will learn them" (38). They also educate her about the rest of Jimmy's customs—she must wear Jimmy's hat and broken watch, and "you will eat the fish, and then you will say the stories of Crake" (39).

The rest of the enclave is waiting for Zeb's search party, who are out searching for Adam One, and also waiting for any remaining God's Gardeners to return. It seems Toby has been attracted to Zeb for some time now. However, there were only a few hints of closeness between them in *The Year of the Flood*. In that novel, when Zeb is injured in a street fight, Toby is one of the only people he wants around him "because at least she was silent" (*Flood*, 109). When Toby and Ren arrive at the cobb house, she is told that Zeb is still alive but "she also doubts it—it won't really be true until she sees him. Touches him" (*Flood*, 391). When Zeb returns from a trip hunting for Adam One, Ren sees that "Toby's got her arms around him," although Toby quickly releases him so Zeb can greet Ren (*Flood*, 397). While Toby waits for him to return from this search mission, she thinks about how disappointed he will be to learn the Painballers got away because she couldn't kill them on Saint Julian's feast day. She reminds herself that, when he does return, "she'll have to face up once again to the fact that she's neutral territory as far as he's concerned. . . . A trusted comrade and foot soldier: reliable Toby, so competent" (27). The search party returns and informs the rest of the group that they've had no luck in finding anyone, but they do find one of the Gardeners dead—presumably he's been murdered by the Painballers. Once this news is shared, Zeb and Toby retreat to the garden to catch up on each other's news. Toby begins to cry when she tells Zeb of what she perceives as her failure to dispose of the Painballers; now not only are they armed again, they have killed someone else. She unexpectedly finds herself "enfolded" by Zeb and their intimate relationship begins (48). He clearly has been harboring the same feelings as she has.

One of the results of their newfound relationship is that Toby begins to feel jealous about Zeb, something she finds unbecoming in herself. For example, Swift Fox has always flirted indiscriminately with all the men, including Zeb. Now Toby thinks spitefully, "she might as well be flashing a blue bottom, like the Crakers" (89). She immediately scolds herself, saying "stop that, Toby" (89). She recognizes that if they begin infighting, "nursing our minor hatreds, indulging our petty resentments, yelling at one another," they might become "distracted by our darker selves" and thus become vulnerable to the Painballers and other predators. However, her admonition doesn't end her internal uneasiness. One morning she finds herself visiting "the violet biolet" because she is waiting for Swift Fox to finish her breakfast and leave the table before she goes to breakfast (97). She "consciously suppresses the word *slut*: a woman should not use that word about another woman" (97, emphasis in original). She is careful to hide these feelings from Zeb, indeed from everyone. And, she realizes that "she has no claims. If Zeb tumbles into bed with Swift Fox . . . what she is entitled to say about that is exactly nothing" (97). Swift Fox herself also obviously feels jealous of Toby's and Zeb's relationship. One morning during breakfast, she directs some "snide innuendoes" at Toby, who responds by feeling "a rush of anger" which, as usual, she works to hide (143).

When a small group of men, including Zeb, decide to take "a quick scan around the area" and ask if anyone needs anything from the abandoned stores, Swift Fox decides that she's going too (143). This reaction surprises everyone and is not received favorably by the scouting party, including Zeb, who says it is a "bad plan" (144), but Swift Fox insists, saying she needs to get "girl stuff" and that she's "gleaning" for some of the other women too (143). Toby, too, is unhappy about the plan, thinking that "she wants to put some sort of mark on [Zeb]. *Mine. Stay away*," but immediately thinks she would "make a fool of herself" (145). Toby spends her day in productive work, but the search party's return is delayed, and her mind immediately moves to worst-case scenarios: what if Zeb "were suddenly not there" (150)? Or even worse: "You've lost Zeb. By now Swift Fox must already have him, firmly clamped in her arms and legs and whatever orifices appeal" (151). She immediately chastises herself, reminding herself that they made no promises to one another. Finally, late the next day, the search party returns. They've come back with a haul of goods (including, Swift Fox says, pregnancy tests); they explain that they were delayed because they were trapped by a group of pigoons. The next morning, they investigate a fire they had seen the night before, believing it must be made by the Painballers, but the men are gone.

Toby is relieved that Zeb and the others are back safely, but she is frustrated that he disappears after his shower and doesn't join her in bed that night. Again, she scolds herself, "no sulking allowed . . . no wound-licking" (158). When he seeks her out in the garden the next day, she reminds herself that "she can't ask what happened with Swift Fox, or if anything did: she refuses to sound like a shrew" (159). Zeb shows her a shoe he found that looks like a Gardener shoe; they both assume it must come from Adam One or any other "surviving Gardeners" (160). Zeb also has gifts for her, including a mirror and some paper and writing utensils, both things she wanted but hadn't told him she did. It seems they are more tightly connected than their nonchalant and cavalier attitudes suggest.

Life goes on as before and the Crakers continue to want stories about Zeb. Zeb, however, senses something is wrong with Toby and asks, "something else eating you?" (219). Toby denies it and he goes on "let me guess. You think I should tell you what happened out in the wilds of the shopping strip with what's-her-name. Little Miss Fox. Whether I groped her or vice versa. Whether sexual congress took place" (220). Toby considers carefully whether she does, in fact, want this information and surprises Zeb by not taking the bait, saying instead, "tell me something more interesting" (220). She tries to resign herself to not know what, if anything, happened between the two of them. In some ways, Atwood is reinforcing cultural beliefs and assumptions about the inevitability of women competing over men, but she also shows Toby struggling to resist her feelings, thus challenging the way this belief has been naturalized or made normative.

Zeb and Toby don't talk explicitly about their feelings for one another, which is part of the reason Toby continues to question what kind of relationship they have and why she is susceptible to jealousy. However, at one point Zeb inadvertently reassures her by telling her that "I'm loyal. To whoever I'm with, if I'm really with them" (230). Toby seems reluctant to embrace this attitude, wondering whether she believes him; at the moment, "she isn't sure" (230).

As all of this is going on, the humans in the enclave continue to engage in building, making, and survival tasks: expanding and fortifying the cobb house, reinforcing the fencing, preparing food. Toby thinks "what to eat, where to shit, how to take shelter, who and what to kill: are these the basics?" She wonders if they've "come down to; or else come back to" this state of affairs (98). Toby also notices that the humans, including herself, are developing a tendency to "drift," as well as "slacking off," which she attributes to the fact that "they have no festivals, no calendars, no deadlines. No long-term goals" (136), nothing except the struggle for survival to ground them. It causes Toby some concern, because she experienced this "floating mood" before, during her time "holed up in the AnooYoo Spa" (136). There she responded by sticking "to her daily routine (136). Now she finds herself "counting heads each morning, making sure all the MaddAddamites and former Gardeners are still in place" (136).

In this novel, too, Atwood reflects on the power of story and narrative. Toby thinks "there's the story, then there's the real story, then there's the story of how the story came to be told. Then there's what you leave out of the story. Which is part of the story too" (56). Each evening the Crakers expect to hear Toby's stories, which she must craft carefully using only the literal language the Crakers understand—no metaphors or abstract concepts. At one point, her stories move away from the creation stories Jimmy developed; the next story the Crakers have decided they are interested in is one about Zeb's past and, in particular, they "want to hear the story of Zeb. And the bear. The bear he ate" (53). Toby questions Zeb about his past to mine material for her stories for them. She realizes that "the Crakers have constructed a formidable set of beliefs about Zeb" (94); they believe him to be very powerful. The story about the bear helps to reinforce that belief. Toby tells Zeb that "they're insatiable on the subject of you" but also wonders about her motivations: "does she want to know about Zeb for the sake of the Crakers, or for herself? Both. But mostly for herself" (106). Toby is always honest with herself about her feelings, even if she doesn't often share them with others.

The bear incident happens during a near-death wilderness survival experience Zeb had while working up north. Doyle calls "the Zeb sections . . . the book's thinnest and pulpiest" and sees Zeb as a caricature, categorizing him as "more or less an archetype: a tough, foul-mouthed, hairy-chested Alpha Dude" ("Dystopia, for the 'Lulz'"). But Zeb's history is significant because his "flashback story, narrated by him, . . . provides the readers with crucial information about Zeb, his brother Adam, and his reasons for establishing the God's Gardeners, as well as about Glenn / Crake, who appears in them as a young boy" (Kuźnicki, *Margaret Atwood's Dystopian Fiction*, 165). These stories are how we as readers learn Zeb's history. Pressing him for details and narratives to retell to the Crakers, Toby discovers that Zeb and Adam One thought they were stepbrothers; they later learn they are not. Their father, the Rev, was the leader of a megachurch with a theology based on oil, The Church of PetrOleum. He's a fraud and hypocrite; he also physically abuses Zeb until Zeb grows big enough to hit back. The Rev is raising substantial sums "skimming the cash from the faithful 24/7" (117), much of which finds its way into his own secret offshore account. As part of his revenge on his father for filling his childhood with mental and physical abuse, Zeb finds his way into the accounts and diverts a small undetectable percentage of the donations to his own secret account; he has become a master coder and "could play code the way Mozart played the piano" (119). Zeb and Adam "plan to disappear from the Rev's charmed circle once they had sufficient funds" (121). When Adam tells Zeb that the Rev killed Adam's mother and she's buried in the garden, they decide the time is right to escape. After cleaning out one of the Rev's more lucrative accounts, they leave town, sending messages to the Rev telling him they know of the murder, the financial fraud, and the Rev's addiction to violent internet porn. They are hopeful that the threat of these details being made public will deter the Rev from trying to come after them.

Because the Rev has significant high-level contacts, they take precautions not to be traced, on- or off-line. They separate, change their appearances, arrange for a secret on-line way to keep in touch, and create alternate identities. Zeb flees to San Jose where he "kept a low profile, stayed out of bars, and blended himself into the underclass" (131) by working a series of different jobs. Eventually Adam contacts him and places him inside HelthWyzer; Zeb poses as a data inputter. This is where Zeb meets Glenn, who has not yet become Crake, and teaches him how to code. Telling this story to Toby, Zeb thinks: "It was a lot of fun watching the kid soak it all up, and who was to foresee the consequences?" (238). Zeb meets Pilar during this time in the compound as well; she is undercover on behalf of Adam and the God's Gardeners. When she is notified that she's being transferred, Pilar arranges for Zeb to leave the compound and smuggle out some pills which are "vectors for bioforms" (247). They are hidden in a chess piece which he is to deliver to a mysterious contact. He is instructed to assume yet another new identity and become a bouncer at Scales and Tails.

When Zeb delivers the pills, he is surprised to see that Adam has shown up to receive them. This is when HelthWyzer's nefarious plans and business practices again are highlighted, as Crake shared with Jimmy in *Oryx and Crake* and Pilar shared with Toby in *The Year of the Flood*: "They're using their vitamin supplement pills and over-the-counter painkillers as vectors for diseases—ones for which they control the drug treatments.... They make money all ways: on the vitamins, then on the drugs, and finally on the hospitalization when the illness takes firm hold" (254).

The pills remain hidden at Scales and Tails until the Rev comes in with some OilCorps colleagues. Because Zeb is in disguise, he remains unrecognized by the Rev and manages to administer three of the pills to him in a drink, causing his father's gruesome death. Zeb is tasked to convey the remains to "the cryptic team" on the West Coast so they can discover what was in the pills. He is then assigned to the janitorial staff as a "Disinfector" (324) on the night shift at another HelthWyzer compound, which gives him an opportunity to snoop until a computer he's hacking "had an alarm on it" (325) and puts him in jeopardy. Zeb joins Adam at God's Gardeners, where Zeb becomes Adam Seven. We know some of the rest of his story from *The Year of the Flood*.

Ivory Bill has been pondering some of the unexpected actions of the Crakers, noting that "their brains are more malleable than Crake intended. They've been doing several things we didn't anticipate during the construction phase" (273). Jimmy observed this earlier, in *Oryx and Crake*, when the Crakers performed the ritual of calling him back to the shore. Perhaps one example of this is that Blackbeard, one of the Craker children, attaches himself to Toby, exhibiting affection and loyalty, characteristics that have not yet been seen among the Crakers. He accompanies her when she checks on Jimmy; he comes to let her know the day that Jimmy is waking up. Toby begins to teach him to read and write, skills he quickly picks up. He appoints himself her "helper" (375).

It turns out Blackbeard can also communicate with the pigoons, who he refers to as "The Pig Ones" (266). It seems to be some kind of telepathic connection, as with the Crakers' earlier connection to Jimmy while he was in his coma. This fluency comes in handy when a delegation of pigoon families, bearing a dead piglet, comes to ask for help from the humans to stop "those ones who are killing their pig babies" (269), in Blackbeard's translation. When the delegation is first seen by the humans, Jimmy says "Oh fuck," which Blackbeard is very happy about, saying "thank you for calling him Snowman-the-Jimmy! We will need him to help us" (266). The pigoons want the "three bad men" (270) killed. Then, if the humans agree to stop killing pigoons, the pigoons will stop eating their garden and won't pose a threat to any of them in the future. Here is perhaps the clearest example that the pigoons can think like humans: they have identified a problem that is a threat to their survival; mapped out a solution; and come to seek allies, demonstrating the ability to reason through a complex thought process. Although there is no overt discussion among the humans of whether to help the pigoons, the pigoons themselves leave because "something appears to have been concluded" (271). Plans to deal with the Painballers proceed.

This communication and ultimate agreement between the pigoons and the humans and Crakers suggest new possibilities for cross-species relationships. In fact, Kuźnicki asserts that this "discovery of a given species' uniqueness and validity, . . . is the key to humanity's survival. It becomes clear that the success of a new world in which these two animals can live side by side depends on their mutual cooperation and trust" (*Margaret Atwood's Dystopian Fiction*, 171). Initially the humans see the pigoons as vicious, violent dangers: when Jimmy's father takes him to visit their pen, he tells Jimmy not to fall in because "they'll eat you up in a minute" (26). When a group of pigoons traps Jimmy in the watchtower during his visit to the Paradice Dome, he calls them "cunning, so cunning" (*Oryx and Crake*, 270). In *The Year of the Flood*, after Toby shoots the pigoon boar, she experiences the pigoons' ability to seek revenge and to grieve. These moments seem to indicate that the pigoons possess something like human feelings. In *MaddAdam*, the pigoons bargain for help and begin to seem more like allies. It's not entirely clear whether the pigoons possessed these qualities all along or whether they are just highly adaptive and quick to learn. In the end, it doesn't matter—the humans and pigoons have arranged to coexist with one another.

In addition to the human / pigoon détente, there are other signs of hope for humanity in *MaddAddam*. Amanda is pregnant. The enclave's assumption is that the father of Amanda's baby must be one of the Painballers who raped her over and over again. Toby, though, wonders if the father might be a Craker who might have impregnated Amanda when four of the men accosted her after she was liberated. Amanda is distraught, but the Craker women are delighted. When the humans convene a group meeting to discuss the situation, they learn that in addition to Amanda's pregnancy, Ren and Swift Fox are also pregnant. Ren knows from her menstrual cycle that her baby wasn't fathered by a Painballer. Swift Fox announces that she can rule out the possibility of a Painballer father; she "can rule out a few other guys, too" (274). However, the father of her baby could also be a Craker.

As some members of the enclave prepare to deal with the Painballers once and for all, the humans realize that some of the group, and in particular the three pregnant women, will be left vulnerable. Even though Swift Fox insists that "we're not just packages, . . . We can fight back!" (274), ultimately it is decided to "move our whole group out of here when we go hunting for those guys" (275). The decision is made: the humans and Crakers will relocate to the AnooYoo Spa where there are "doors that lock" (275); it is significantly more secure than they are able to make the cobb house compound. Two pigoons escort them; the other pigoons will meet them at the Spa.

As everyone gets settled at AnooYoo, Zeb and Toby begin to open up with one another about their feelings. Toby shares that while she was living there before she nursed Ren and they found the human / Craker enclave, she was waiting for Zeb. She had confidence that "if anyone knew how to stay alive through all of that, it would be you" (293). He allows himself to become vulnerable in return, asking whether she thought the wait was worth it. Toby is incredulous, asking "you're having a failure of confidence? You need to ask?" (293). When he is later recounting more of his story and, in particular, how he ended up at the Garden with Lucerne and Ren, he explains that Lucerne wanted to "go through the God's Gardeners Partnership ceremony with him;" he refused, finding it "a meaningless empty symbol" (332). For this ceremony, the couple "jumped over a bonfire together and then traded green branches while everyone stood in a circle" (332). Possibly the ceremony was loosely inspired by the African-American tradition during slavery of jumping the broom in place of a marriage ceremony, which was illegal for African-American couples. Some pagan handfasting ceremonies also involve a broom. Toby is surprised when Zeb then suggests that "if we both come out of this tomorrow, maybe we should do the bonfire thing. With the green branches" (335). She can't quite take him seriously, although they do in fact go through the ceremony later, something Blackbeard finds "strange" (379).

The pigoon scouts tell them that the Painballers are headed in the direction of the Paradice Dome. A third man with them is injured; he does indeed turn out to be Adam One. While planning the tracking mission, the question of "who comes with us, who stays here" is raised (342). Zeb insists that Blackbeard also join the group. Toby is opposed to this plan, thinking that "she doesn't think she could live with herself if little Blackbeard got killed" (343). Although it's possible she might feel like this about any child, there is a special closeness between Blackbeard and Toby, rooted in Toby's role as his teacher, the amount of time they spend together, and Blackbeard's clear affection for Toby. Blackbeard solves the dispute for them by saying that "I need to come, the Pig Ones have said so" (343). He also shares that "Oryx will be helping me, and Fuck. I have already called Fuck, he is flying to here, right now. You will see" (343). Surprisingly, Jimmy insists on coming as well. Toby and Zeb don't think this is wise, based on his injured foot and recent illness, but Jimmy notes that "I know where everything is. Such as the cellpacks. And the sprayguns" (344). Jimmy wins this argument, but Zeb threatens that if Jimmy can't keep up, he'll be sent back under pigoon escort.

As they begin the journey, the pigoons assign "three guards to each of the gunbearers" (348). The pigoon scouts continue to feed intelligence to the group through their mysterious interactions with Blackbeard. It turns out that Jimmy, in fact, is not in good enough shape for the journey although he continues to refuse to return to the Spa. The pigoons come to the rescue: one carries Jimmy on his back and one pigoon accompanies them on each side to keep him from falling off. The pigoons are excellent guides; once in the RejoovenEsense Compound, Jimmy is disoriented, but they "are sure of the trail" (351). The pigoons also enter the Dome to secure the door to the storage unit where the sprayguns are stored, blocking it so the Painballers can't get in.

After the corpses of Oryx and Crake are discovered in the dome, the action that follows is relayed in an evening story to the Crakers, the Story of the Battle. In an unusual twist, Blackbeard is the one who tells it, as Toby is "too sad, because of the dead ones" (357). He explains that Toby and the others, including the Pig Ones, have to deal with the bad men because otherwise the rest of them would continue to be in danger. During their visit to the Dome, Blackbeard is distraught when he discovers the site of what remains of Oryx and Crake. As he relates this to the Crakers, he shares Toby's comments that "the bone piles were not the real Oryx and Crake any more, they were only husks like an eggshell" (359), an explanation that seems to reassure both Blackbeard and, later, the rest of the Crakers. Once discovered, the Painballers try to use the injured Adam as a bargaining chip so they can escape with the sprayguns, but Adam signals the group not to agree. In the ensuing gun battle, Adam is killed and Jimmy and the two Painballers are badly injured. Several of the Pig Ones are injured and one has died. Jimmy dies on their way back to the cobb house.

The humans hold a sort of trial to decide what to do with the Painballers. There is no question about their actions and their guilt; "the trial is about the verdict only" (367). Surprisingly, the group is not in agreement about whether to kill them. Ivory Bill suggests they think about "correctional guardianship," and White Sedge suggests that "we could try rehabilitation" (369). No one else agrees with either idea. After the vote, the verdict is clear: death to the Painballers. The Pig Ones want them dead also, according to Blackbeard. The Pig Ones join Zeb and Toby and several of the other humans in taking the Painballers to the shore to execute them. Toby forbids the Crakers to go, because "it would be hurtful to us" (370). It might also be that since the Crakers released the men the first time they were captured, and, even though they've been told the men are a danger to the humans as well as the Crakers, she is worried about what they might do at the moment of execution.

After the group returns, the pigoons reaffirm their agreement not to harm the enclave and to leave their gardens and bees alone. Toby reaffirms the pact on the human side. Although Blackbeard has already told the story of the trial, Toby recounts the aftermath of the execution in her journal. The pigoons help them transport Adam and Jimmy to the burial site, where Pilar is also buried. As part of their process for moving on, the Crakers "made the pictures of Snowman-the-Jimmy and of Adam" (376). These pictures are symbolic representations of the dead men, made with detritus from the shore and the enclave. This scene evokes memories of when they "made a picture of Snowman-the-Jimmy once before, to call him back, and it did call him back" from one of his earlier trips to the Dome (376). Blackbeard is aware that the pictures won't have the same effect this time but feels that the process comforts the other Crakers.

The final chapters of the novel alternate between Blackbeard's voice—both telling stories to the Crakers and writing in his own journal—and Toby's journal entries. The Compound is thriving: the garden is growing, the flock of Mo'Hairs is growing, and there are three more solar units. A brief garden incursion by two young pigoons has the potential to derail their mutual agreement to nondestruction. However, adult pigoons arrive in embarrassment to assure the enclave that it won't happen again and proceed to issue severe threats to their offspring.

All the babies are successfully delivered. Swift Fox's twins are Craker / human hybrids, as are Amanda's. Different enclave men take primary responsibility for assisting the mothers and their babies, in effect serving as co-parents. There is real curiosity in the enclave about what these children might be like. In addition to their green Craker eyes, "what other features might these children have inherited? Will they have built-in insect repellent, or the unique focal structures that enable purring and Craker singing? Will they share the Craker sexual cycles?" (380). All of this is yet to be determined, but the children are yet another manifestation of the possibilities of cross-species relationships. Kuźnicki suggests that "the three pregnancies and their outcomes are presented as the first manifestations of a new life that is born within the MaddAddamite group in the post-apocalyptic world characterized by destruction and death" (*Margaret Atwood's Dystopian Fiction,* 182). It also suggests that there is hope for human survival in what continues to be a difficult environment, as well as hope in and for the future.

Blackbeard continues to write the narrative of the compound in his journal. He becomes the keeper of the stories and the histories. He also teaches the Craker / hybrid children to read and write. It is not clear why he doesn't teach other Crakers at this time as well, but he has instructed the hybrid children that after he dies, they are to teach other young ones to read and write. Toby has instructed Blackbeard not only to continue to write, but also to make or have made multiple copies of the journal, so the stories are preserved, possibly indicating her belief—or at least her hope—that human civilization will survive. When Blackbeard is showing the "Book that Toby made" he notes that it includes "the Words of Fuck, though these Words are not very long" and explains: "Yes, I know he helps us when we are in trouble, and comes flying. He was sent by Crake, and we speak his name in Crake's honour. But there is not very much about him in writing" (386).

In the final pages of the book, Blackbeard tells more about Toby. While out hunting, Zeb sees smoke from a small fire and organizes a scouting trip to investigate who is at the fire and to ascertain "would they be good people, or would they be bad and cruel men" (388). They do not return, and a second scouting trip discovers that the fire is not there any longer. Toby mourns Zeb deeply and, as Blackbeard says, is "more sad than anyone" (389). Toby also becomes ill with "a wasting sickness" (389). In an echo of Pilar's earlier determination about when and how she would die, Toby also claims the right to decide when and how her death would happen. She leaves the compound to go into the forest with the poisonous herbs and mushrooms and there she dies.

The novel ends by emphasizing and reaffirming the possibility of continuing survival. Swift Fox is pregnant again; the fathers are Crakers, including Blackbeard. She has promised that "if it was a girl baby, it would be named Toby;" Blackbeard notes that "that is a thing of hope" (390). The growing enclave and the mutually beneficial relationship between the humans and the pigoons point very strongly to hope and possibility—or at the very least, survival. But that hope is not unqualified. Although Zeb is presumed dead, whoever built the fire that alerted him that there were other humans alive are still out there somewhere in the world. Thus, the novel's conclusion is ambiguous.

MaddAddam, too, has received varying critical evaluations. Wisker attributes that, at least in part, to "its post-apocalyptic, sustainability theme, and its mixture of the homey arts and crafts, its quasi-religious tone, and its sometimes cartoonish characters" (*Margaret Atwood*, 176), suggesting that some find this juxtaposition unsuccessful. In a review written a decade before sharing the Booker Prize with Atwood, Bernardine Evaristo is less than enthusiastic about the novel, finding that "character, it seems, has been sacrificed at the altar of this speculative universe" ("The Year of the Flood"). However, Michiko Kakutani applauds that Atwood has "given her imagination free rein;" in contrast, Kakutani found *Oryx and Crake* "lumpy" ("A Familiar Cast").

Bland argues compellingly that the trilogy is "one of the most impressive achievements in contemporary literature . . . a grand document of humanity's greatest failings but also a moving celebration of our greatest possibilities" ("It's 'Scary'"). The novel has also made an impact on media outside literature. In a podcast interview with *The Geek's Guide to the Galaxy*, Atwood shares that some coders have made one of the video games in *MaddAddam*, *Intestinal Parasites*,[3] into an actual video game ("Interview"). And, as mentioned earlier, the trilogy has been optioned for a TV series.

Stein argues that Atwood "holds out hope that apocalyptic fictions such as hers may lead readers to imagine more favorable future scenarios and therefore to practice more egalitarian and ecofriendly behaviors that will avert ecological disasters" ("Surviving the Waterless Flood," 313). No reader can doubt that this would be an admirable goal.

CHAPTER 5

The Heart Goes Last
Desperation and Possibility

The Heart Goes Last (2015) began as a serial titled "Positron," published on the now-defunct platform Byliner; excerpts of the novel were also published on Wattpad. This novel tells the stories of Charmaine and Stan, currently poor and homeless, who accept an offer to live at Consilience, a model town that is part of the Positron Project. Purportedly designed to solve societal problems, Positron is an ominous example of the surveillance state, with resistance from the inside and pressure from outside forces concerned about its actions. As with all Atwood's novels, this text is a response to a question. Here the question is "How much social instability would it take before people would renounce their hard-won civil liberties in a tradeoff for 'safety'?" (Howells, "True Trash," 305).

The novel encompasses multiple genres; M. John Harrison calls it a "jubilant comedy of errors, bizarre bedroom farce, SF prison-break thriller, psychedelic 60s crime caper" ("*The Heart Goes Last*"). Sections of the novel verge on the cartoonish (especially the enormously complicated plot to alert the outside world to what's really happening at Consilience and the use of the almost-farcical Green Men and Elvis Presley and Marilyn Monroe impersonators). Sarah Lyall notes that Atwood has created "an intricate web that ensnares Charmaine and Stan in a dizzying game of betrayal and counterbetrayal involving extramarital affairs, human-organ trafficking, blackmail, espionage, identity theft and sex-bot manufacturing" ("Review").

The novel received widely varying critical responses. Mat Johnson labels it "a captivating jump into the absurdity of dominance and desire, love and independence." Stacey May Fowles describes it as "deeply witty and oddly beautiful" ("Review"). Harrison calls it "a jarring, rewardingly strange piece of work" ("*The Heart Goes Last*"). Anita Sethi says it is a "visceral study of desperation and desire" ("*The Heart Goes Last*"). In 2016 the novel received the Red Tentacle award "for the most 'progressive, intelligent and entertaining' novel of the year" (Flood, "Margaret Atwood Wins Kitchies"). But Lyall finds that the novel "loses control of itself" and "suffers in comparison with [her] previous books" ("Review"). Gretchen Shirm claims that the humor is "strangely crass and the depiction of women troubling" ("*The Heart Goes Last*").

The novel opens with the depressing scene of Stan and Charmaine living in their car after they have lost first their jobs and then their house because of the collapse of the economic system. Charmaine manages to pick up a few shifts a week at Dust, a dive bar that serves as a meeting place for local drug dealers, and it is with that small bit of income that they must survive. It's a dystopic environment, crawling with gangs and vandals, which means they frequently have to flee in the middle of the night and find another place to park their car. Charmaine tries to "look to the bright side" (4) and sprinkles her thoughts with her Grandma Win's clichés, which remind her that "cleanliness is next to godliness" (4) and of the things that "we never appreciated until we didn't have them" (13), among others.

We come to learn that Charmaine lived with her grandmother due to neglect and child abuse in her home, apparently at the hands of her father. This information about Charmaine's history comes out in italicized comments from Grandma Win and her father, which are scattered throughout the novel. Grandma Win advises her to "*try hard to forget those other things, because a man's not accountable when he's had too much to drink*" (5, emphasis in original), a common excuse men use to explain their violence against women.

When Charmaine tries to remember the house she lived in before Grandma Win's, the memory that comes is "*Clean that up! Don't talk back!*' She hadn't talked back—crying wasn't talking—but that hadn't made any difference, she was wrong all the same" (25, emphasis in original). Or, later, "*Come here. Don't think you can hide. Look at me. You're a bad girl, aren't you? No* was the wrong answer to that, but so was *Yes. Stop that noise. Shut up, I said shut up! You don't even know what hurt is*" (24, emphasis in original). Although we know that Charmaine's mother is dead, because Grandma Win has told her that "*your mother didn't kill herself, that was just talk*" (4, emphasis in original), we don't know what the status of her father is. When she and Stan marry, no parents are invited, "their parents being dead one way or another" (6).

These childhood experiences make her particularly sensitive to any anger from Stan. One particularly bad night, when they've had to relocate the car twice because of danger from gangs, Charmaine tries to soothe Stan by saying "Relax a little. Go to sleep. Your brain's too active." His response is cutting: "what fucking brain?"—a response he immediately regrets, even though it's a criticism of himself, as "there's a hurt silence" and he thinks "he shouldn't take it out on her. Dickhead, he tells himself. None of this is her fault" (10). Later in the novel, Charmaine remembers another argument, when Stan was angry because she "*fucking blew*" money on a bottle of nail polish (251, emphasis in original). She actually stands up to him at first this time, arguing that "it was her money, she'd earned it herself" (251). This reply makes him even more angry and he "accused her of throwing it up to him that he didn't have a job, and then she said she was not throwing it up, she only wanted her toes to look nice for him, and he said he didn't give a fucking fuck about her fucking toe colour" (251). When she begins to cry, the argument ends.

At least in part as a result of having to tightly monitor her behavior as a child, Charmaine is a people pleaser. In fact, she even has an "I-am-a-good-person smile" that she consciously and strategically deploys (146). This smile is a large part of what drew Stan to her: "that's why he married her: she was an escape from the many-layered, devious, ironic, hot-cold women he'd tangled himself up with until then; . . . He liked the retro thing about Charmaine, the cookie-ad thing, her prissiness, the way she hardly ever swore" (48). Charmaine is attracted to similar qualities in Stan. They have "a different kind of love. Trusting, sedate . . . She loved Stan because she liked solid ground under her feet, non-reflective surfaces, movies with neat endings" (53), in dramatic opposition to her early childhood. However, despite Charmaine's good girl persona, when Sandi and Veronica, the two prostitutes who work out of Dust, suggest that she might "turn a few," she is at first predictably appalled but then somewhat titillated. She notices that "she'd had a tiny flash of excitement, like peering in through a window and seeing another version of herself inside, leading a second life; a more raucous and rewarding second life. . . . What would it be like? But no, she couldn't because it was way too dangerous" (19). This brief moment of fantasy foreshadows some of Charmaine's future experiences.

One day when Charmaine is working her shift at Dust, she sees a TV ad soliciting members for the Positron Project where there is "not only full employment but also protection from the dangerous elements that afflict so many at this time" (26). The ad shows a beautiful town, inhabited by "young couples, holding hands, energetic and smiling" and lovely homes (25). Charmaine thinks of how their life—now full of deprivation and poverty—could change: "Will there be a washer and dryer in that new home? Of course there will. And a dining table . . . Lunches, intimate dinners, just the two of them.

They'll sit on chairs while eating, they'll have real china instead of plastic. Maybe even candles" (27). She convinces Stan that they should apply to be part of the community.

Stan, Charmaine, and the other applicants are bussed to Consilience. As they are driven through town, "Charmaine says she can hardly believe her eyes: everything is so spruced up, it's like a picture" (32). All the applicants are entertained at "a preliminary drinks and snacks party in the ballroom" of a hotel (32). Stan notes that the crowd shrinks during the party but realizes they "must have passed scrutiny, because here they still are" (32). They are housed at a lovely hotel and given vouchers to a beautiful restaurant. The next day Stan and Charmaine, along with other applicants, sit through a number of presentations designed to show them the happy residents of Consilience. Then the applicants who have made it this far in the process, including Stan and Charmaine, are sent back "outside" (33) for one last opportunity to change their minds. After that, "you were either out or you were in. *In* was permanent. But no one would force you. If you signed up, it would be of your own free will" (33). Despite the choice rhetoric, this seems manipulative as Consilience must be aware of the desperate straits of some of the applicants. The enforced delay seems like a way to assuage their own consciences. Stan and Charmaine have already decided to sign up when Stan's often-estranged, drug-dealing brother Conor shows up at their hotel with some dark warnings: "Don't trust that package, no matter what they tell you," and "You don't know what goes on in there" (35). Stan's response is "meaning what? Meaning you do?" Conor explains that "I've heard stuff . . . It's not for you. Nice guys finish last. Or else they get finished. You're too soft" (35). Later in the novel, readers discover who he may have "heard stuff" from.

In spite of Conor's warnings, Stan and Charmaine sign the documents to join Consilience. As Fowles notes, "Atwood does an excellent job of convincing us that we, too, would do the same if we were in their shoes" ("Review"). After finishing their paperwork, they are told more about the project and their future. Allegedly designed to address the current social unrest and destitution of so many, the "Consilience/Positron twin city is an experiment . . . [with] unemployment and crime solved in one fell swoop" (37). This desirable outcome is achieved after discovering that "if prisons were scaled out and handled rationally, they could be win–win viable economic units" (40). To manage this, "everyone in Consilience will live two lives: prisoners one month, guards or town functionaries the next" (42); the prison is also called Positron. They will share their houses with "Alternates" (42), couples who are in prison when they are out and vice versa. The town intentionally recreates the feel of the 1950s "because that was the decade in which the most people had self-identified as being happy" (41). Of course, scholarship on the actual 1950s demonstrates the ways in which that decade has been romanticized. Some people were happy and economically comfortable in that decade, primarily middle- to upper class white men, and sometimes white women (although Betty Friedan's *The Feminine Mystique* speaks to the real discontent of many, mostly white women). After moving into their very own house, Charmaine is elated, although eventually she comes to recognize that "citizens were always a bit like inmates and inmates were always a bit like citizens, so Consilience and Positron have only made it official" (145). Stan, on the other hand, "can't shake the feeling that this place is some sort of pyramid scheme" (44); once inside Positron he begins to think (accurately) that "some folks must be making a shitload of cash out of this thing" (81). It is not clear at this stage of the novel how, in fact, the project was financed in the beginning or who is benefiting financially from it and how.

Stan is given a job repairing scooters; in jail he maintains the software that runs the poultry house. When they're outside, Charmaine works at a bakery and, in the prison, as the Chief Medications Administrator, a job title and responsibility that brings her pride. Stan comes to realize that, although they are safe and their basic needs are met in Consilience, he wants more passion in his life than the predictability of the prison / outside routine. He is dissatisfied with their sex life, thinking that "it's not that they don't have sex. They certainly have more of it than they had in the car; but it's sex that Charmaine enacts, like yoga, with careful breath control. What he wants is sex that can't be helped. . . . No no no, yes yes yes! That's what he wants" (45). On the other hand, Charmaine seems quite content since "having two lives means there's always something different to look forward to" (50), indicating, perhaps, that she enjoys the change of routine each month. Soon she has something else to look forward to.

When Stan discovers a note under their refrigerator to Max from Jasmine, he believes he's discovered the identities of their alternates. The note is intimate, passionate, and sensual, complete with a fuchsia lipstick kiss; Sam begins to obsess about the note and its writer, wishing again that Charmaine would exhibit such intense desire for him. He projects his own fantasies on to Max and Jasmine, extending his wish for Charmaine to exhibit uncontrollable need for him. Stan imagines the moment when Max and Jasmine encounter each other after their month in prison (the prison is segregated by gender): "Jasmine will throw herself into Max's arms, press herself against him, open her fuchsia mouth, tear off Max's clothes and her own" (47). One of his goals becomes "the discovering and seduction of Jasmine" (61).

While Stan is trying to figure out how he can meet Jasmine, Charmaine, who *is* actually Jasmine, is having an affair with Max. The two of them meet one changeover day when he comes to the house before she's left for the prison; he immediately spirits her off to an uninhabited house to have sex. Because of Max's job with the Reclamation Team, he knows where there are vacant houses for their trysts. It's not at all clear why Charmaine succumbs to him this first time; most women would be terrified by a complete stranger entering their bedroom and beginning to undress them. However, during their sexual encounters, Charmaine/Jasmine is completely uninhibited, unlike the sexual behavior Stan has described. She finds herself "swept away. Drugged with desire. Like a cyclone. Helpless moaning. All of that. She'd never known about such a force, such an energy inside herself. She'd thought it was only in books and TV, or else for other people" (53). Max likes her to talk dirty: *"Now I'm gonna make you say something better with your slutty purple mouth Ask me for it. Bend over"* (58, emphasis in original). Charmaine finds it difficult to believe that she uses such language so easily, musing about saying "words she never would have used before. Vandal words. Sometimes she can't believe what comes out of her mouth; not to mention what goes into it. She does whatever Max wants" (84). In this split personality, "Charmaine/Jasmine functions within the Madonna/whore paradigm" (Cannella, "Feminine Subterfuge," 18). Ironically, Charmaine as Jasmine is the woman about whom Stan is fantasizing.

At one point, Charmaine realizes that Stan must have read the note she left for Max, the one with her Purple Passion lipstick kiss. She notices that Stan's personality changes after she left the note; he "has been so preoccupied he might as well be deaf and blind" (57). Shortly thereafter when they are having sex, Stan says to her "just fucking let go!" (57). He also once accidentally calls her Jasmine, which she ignores and pretends not to have heard. Charmaine thinks that "she needs to break it off with Max" (57). But she doesn't.

Stan soon comes up with a plan to locate Jasmine by installing an illicit cell phone in the seat of the scooter she and Charmaine share. (As with the house and its furnishings, the Alternates share the scooters with their counterparts.) In an uncanny parallel to what has happened and is happening between Max and Charmaine, he imagines encountering Jasmine on switchover day and thinks, "before she knows it, he'll have his mouth on those cherry-flavoured lips, and she'll crumple; she won't be able to resist, any more than paper can resist a lit match" (72); this seems to be a bit of an embellishment, as there is no evidence that the purple lipstick is flavored, but that may be a small quibble. Howells describes this subplot as a "narrative of fantasies and doubles [which] plays out as edgy comedy that frequently spills over into bedroom farce" ("True Trash," 306). Throughout this fantasy, Stan seems to have no sense of or interest in Jasmine as a person, but only considers what she could offer him: hot, passionate sex. He also has no apparent worry about what his infidelity would do to Charmaine—and at this point, he doesn't know she has been unfaithful to him.

Charmaine continues to worry that Stan suspects something and wonders "what if Stan really does know?" (74). She has observed that "Stan's been looking at her, or rather looking through her, as if she's made of glass. That's scarier than if he'd been crabby or angry, or outright accused her" (74). She doesn't know for certain what has caused this change, but she does know Max discovered the note in a location slightly different from where she left it. She thinks about what she would do if Stan became violent, and wonders if "she saved just a little [fatal medication] from each Procedure vial," accessible because of her role as Chief Medications Administrator, could she inject him while he is asleep? Charmaine immediately dismisses the thought, reminding herself that she loves him (76). In fact, because of the tracking device Stan installed on her scooter, he has discovered her visits "to the seedier part of town, where the unreclaimed houses are located" (80), although he hasn't yet discovered why she was there. On the next switchover day, he plans to intercept the female Alternate who lives in their house during Stan and Charmaine's prison times (the woman who he thinks is Jasmine); instead she surprises him in the garage where he is watching for her. Married to Max, who is really Phil, Jocelyn "describes to him in way too much detail the movements of Charmaine on switchover days" (84). Stan is outraged at Charmaine, fuming "how dare she show herself to be everything he was so annoyed with her for not being?" (85).

Jocelyn works in Surveillance and has "rearranged the data" so Phil goes to prison this month in Stan's place (95); she has also arranged for Charmaine to be out of the way. Jocelyn suggests that "we can have a twosome of our own" (86) and reveals that there are cameras in the unreclaimed houses that Max / Phil and Jasmine / Charmaine have been using for their trysts; she has the videos of Charmaine having sex with Max. In part, this adds to Stan's fury at Charmaine, seeing that she "required nothing more than a closed door and a bare floor to release her inner sidewalk whore and urge Phil to do things she'd never allowed Stan to do and say things she'd never once said to Stan" (99). In a twisted expression of apparent desire, Jocelyn insists that Stan watch the videos with her and, then, "she wants him to re-create these videos, playing Phil, with her in the role of Charmaine" (99); he feels like "an indentured studmuffin" (101). She insists that he repeat Phil's dialogue and she responds with Charmaine's words; "she wanted what Charmaine had right there onscreen, and not a syllable less" (108). And, in an eerie echo of Stan asking Charmaine to "just fucking let go!" (57), one night Jocelyn says to him "Just imagine I'm Jasmine, . . . Just let yourself go" (102). Lyall argues that here the novel becomes "a strange quasi-sex romp concerned almost exclusively with erotic power, kinky impulses and the perversity of desire" ("Review"). It's unclear at this point what Jocelyn's motives are; she might be jealous because of Phil's infidelities and wants revenge.

The story rapidly gets even more convoluted, with multiple layers of plots, plans, and deceptions; Sethi calls it "increasingly bizarre" (*The Heart Goes Last*). As part of Charmaine's job in jail, she is required to perform what are euphemistically termed secret "Special Procedure[s]" (67), but the reality is that she euthanizes people. She's told that it's "the troublemakers" who are chosen for the Procedure and that "It's a last resort" (69), which she finds convenient to believe. Charmaine tries to make the patients' last minutes comforting, and "hopes she appears to [them] like an angel: an angel of mercy" (69). After she administers the drug, Charmaine describes the results. First "he's unconscious. Then he stops breathing. The heart goes last" (70). She is not "to tell anyone what she's actually doing, not even Stan" (69), an order she follows.

At the end of one of the months in prison, Charmaine is summoned by Human Resources. She's very worried, wondering if they know about Max, which would be forbidden "because how many times were they told it was absolutely not allowed to fraternize with the Alternates who shared" their house (87). Then she wonders if "they've decided she's being too nice to the subjects during the Special Procedures . . . with the little touches she's added because it makes the whole thing a more quality experience, not only for the subject of the Procedure but for herself as well" (87). These "little touches" hint that she might actually have some reservations about being an angel of mercy and being responsible for killing people without really knowing why.

Aurora from Human Resources arrives to tell her that she "must stay in Positron Prison for another month. In addition to that, she's been relieved of her duties with Medications Administration" (95); she's been reassigned to Towel-Folding. There is apparently some discrepancy with her "data"; "her "codes and cards have been deactivated" temporarily (96). Charmaine finds this troubling and disconcerting. She doesn't know anyone in the knitting circle for this month's prisoners, and they are "making it clear they don't know why she's been stuck in among them" (97). She also isn't given a new roommate, which concerns her; she feels "they're isolating her" (98). Soon Charmaine's identity is "confirmed" and she's restored to her role as Chief Medications Administrator (112). However, because "the synchronization is off" and the Alternates are purportedly living in her house, she is told she has to continue to stay in prison. This situation has no doubt been arranged by Jocelyn, who is "high up in Surveillance" (125), possibly so Jocelyn can continue her sexual adventures with Stan.

During Charmaine's last hours in Towel-Folding before she can resume her former role, Ed, the head of Consilience, appears with Lucinda Quant, a TV personality. Charmaine is star-struck, recognizing Quant from a TV show she used to watch when she and Stan still had their house (and a TV). Quant is considering profiling the Project "so she can tell the world about the wonderful solution we have here, to the problems of homelessness and joblessness," as Ed says (115). This encounter is followed shortly by a Town Meeting where Ed tells everyone how successful Consilience has become and that they are "getting inquiries from other stricken communities, who see the Project as a way of solving their own problems, both economic and social" (117). However, the Project has become "so successful that it has created enemies" (117). There are reporters "trying to worm their way in, to get evidence . . . to turn the outside world against everything the Positron Project stands for" (117). It turns out that Quant herself "had been discovered in the act of taking clandestine pictures intended to present a slanted view" (118). These journalists argue that their attempted exposés are "in the interests of so-called press freedom, and in order to restore so-called human rights, and under the pretense that transparency is a virtue and the people need to know," a position Ed clearly does not agree with (118). There have also been protests on the outside about the project. He warns everyone that "these enemies, if they succeeded, would destroy everyone's job security and very way of life!" thus jeopardizing the safety and stability Stan and Charmaine have found in Consilience (119).

After the Town Hall, Ed visits Charmaine's knitting circle to inform them that "some of those saboteurs have been identified, and they are being brought right here to Positron to be dealt with" (122). They are not to interact with "those new-style prisoners" and "any unusual sounds are to be ignored" (122); this instruction is followed by an unidentified scream. And, unfortunately, Ed continues, Positron Prison "will become a less trusting and open place, because that is what happens in a crisis" (122). In a conversation between Stan and Jocelyn after the Town Hall, Stan discovers that at least part of Jocelyn's motivation for their bizarre relationship was that she was evaluating him for a task. She says approvingly: "by the way, you kept your cool very well during our time together. I know I'm not your favourite squeeze toy, but you would have fooled most. Which is why I'm asking you to do this: because I think you can" (125). She then tells Stan that she is actually one of the saboteurs Ed has warned about at the Town Meeting. She tells Stan the real story about Consilience—a large part of their profit comes from "body parts" because "there's a big market for transplant materials" (126). Ed is bringing in "undesirables" to supply the body parts; these are no doubt the new kind of prisoners Ed told

Charmaine's group about. In addition, they are branching out into "babies' blood" which is said to be "very rejuvenating for the elderly, and the margin on that is going to be astronomical" (127). As in some of the other novels, readers again see Atwood's concern with the misuse of science or the unethical behavior of scientists, extending the concerns about bioengineering she foregrounded in the *MaddAddam* trilogy.

Presumably these things trouble Jocelyn, too, which is why she is trying to destroy the Project. This is the real reason Ed's worried about security and saboteurs. Stan sees evidence of this revised approach when he sees the first load of the new prisoners on his way to work; they're "wearing the regulation orange boiler suits, but they're hooded, their hands plasticuffed behind their backs" (120). Stan recognizes immediately the reason the new prisoners are being delivered so publicly: "No need to parade them like this unless it's a demonstration, . . . A demonstration of power" (120). It's a clear warning to Consilience residents to conform and not to endanger the Project.

Jocelyn wants to smuggle Stan out of the Project with "a digitized document dump and some videos, on a flash drive" (127). He'll be, Stan notes, "the errand boy" (127). Jocelyn lays out the plan. She's going to have Stan "eliminated." If anyone is "checking up on" her, "they'll see how I'd be tempted to use my own power for personal reasons" (129). The personal reasons that provide Jocelyn with a motive for having him murdered are Phil's affair with Charmaine, and Jocelyn's "degrading and jealous attempts to re-enact that affair and punish Charmaine" through Stan (129). This rationale is far from convincing. Surely her sexual encounters with Stan in his guise as Phil, and her pretense at being Charmaine, do not show her in any favorable light. She also tells him that, if needed, "those who might have to be shown those videos will see why I might want to get rid of you" (130) and they would understand why she would need to involve Charmaine who "filched my husband" (130). Accordingly, Stan learns that what Charmaine really does in Medications Administration is perform the Special Procedures. He is in disbelief that Charmaine is "a murderess" (130). Stan professes to believe that Charmaine won't kill him, since she won't be told about the plot and will think she really is murdering him, "but he's not completely sure of that any more" (131). Jocelyn drugs Stan and, when he awakens, he's restrained and "strapped down" (135).

At the same time, Charmaine is eagerly waiting for lunch to be over so she can resume her job doing Special Procedures, although she's a little anxious that she might have "lost her touch" (139). When she goes back to her cell to prepare herself, she discovers a strange woman handcuffed with a hood over her head. She removes the hood and is shocked to see it is Sandi, one of the prostitutes from the Dust. Sandi tells her that they wanted Veronica (the other former prostitute) to kill people; they had clearly been training Veronica to do the Special Procedures. Veronica refused and then disappeared. After that, Sandi tries to escape and is caught. Shortly two guards come to take Sandi away. It shortly becomes very clear "why they put Sandi in her cell: as a warning" (154).

When Charmaine arrives at work to resume her normal duties shortly afterwards, it is Jocelyn's head that appears in the box which is the vehicle through which she is normally given the instructions for her patient. She also informs Charmaine that she is "on probation" and "must undergo a test" (149). It is her loyalty and her "professional dedication" that are being tested (149). Charmaine becomes defensive, indignantly asserting her competence, capabilities, and dependability. Jocelyn warns her that "today, this time, you may encounter a situation that you find challenging. Despite this, the Procedure must be carried out. Your future here depends on it" (149). The alternative is that she can resign and go back to Towel-Folding. Charmaine decides to go forward with the procedure; Jocelyn then reminds her that there "are only two kinds of people admitted to the Medications Administration wing: those who do and those who are done to. You have elected the role of those who do." Then she warns Charmaine that "if you fail, the consequences to yourself will be severe. You may find yourself playing the other role" (150). The threat is clear, particularly after seeing Sandi restrained.

Charmaine goes through the standard routine to get the materials she needs and, when she enters the room, begins with cheerful comments, as was her practice in the past. However, once she sees the patient and realizes that it's Stan, she is horrified and almost falls apart, doubting her ability—or willingness—to continue the procedure. She begins to weep as she thinks of "the two of them when they were first married" and, even during their homelessness period, "they'd stayed together because they had each other and they loved each other" (152). In trying to resolve the moral dilemma she faces, Charmaine steadies herself by telling herself firmly, "don't be sentimental. Remember it's a test" (153). Then she determines that she won't do it but realizes that "the bad thing will happen to him anyway," and the consequences to her will also be significant (154). She proceeds to administer what she believes is a fatal dose and then faints. It is unclear whether Charmaine chose to go forward out of mercy and to save Stan suffering, or out of self-preservation, or both.

After her fall, Charmaine awakens in her own home, mysteriously dressed in her own clothes. Aurora, the representative from human resources, is there and tells her that she is to be taken to the hospital for a CAT scan to rule out a concussion from her fall; a trauma counselor will also be available to her. Aurora also shares that the story being put out about Stan's unexpected death—it was an "electrical accident at the chicken facility" (163). After Aurora leaves, Charmaine begins to tidy the house as a mechanism to calm herself. She notices the light on the DVD player flashing and hits play, only to find that it is a DVD with the footage of her and Max having sex. She hadn't known they were being filmed. She is appalled, wondering who was watching and why.

Jocelyn arrives shortly to escort Charmaine to her CAT scan. Charmaine recognizes her as the talking head in the box who gave her the relevant information for Stan's Special Procedure and told her it was a test. When she says as much to Jocelyn, Jocelyn notes that Charmaine has "had a shock" and is "confused" and says further that "it's normal to blame others. . . . We find it hard to grasp the randomness of the universe" (171), feeding Charmaine the attitude she wants her to display. Charmaine first responds with anger but then thinks that she better "play along, pretend to believe her" because to continue to push might result in negative consequences (171). When they go out to the car, Charmaine is shocked when the driver is Max. He claims his name is Phil and pretends not to know her; Charmaine feels as if she is being gaslit by both Jocelyn and Max. She realizes she must pretend that she believes the narrative about Stan's death, that he died heroically in a fire at the chicken facility; she should "act dumb, because they were messing with her head. . . . it's safer to go along with whatever made-up version of themselves they want to put out there" (181). The need for self-preservation trumps any need to express her feelings.

Aurora insists on staying at the house with Charmaine, purportedly for her own good. Charmaine understands that Aurora's role is to monitor her and, no doubt, to make sure Charmaine doesn't do anything problematic. In a perfectly reasonable reaction to all the recent events, Charmaine can't stop thinking about Stan's death, wondering "why had they wanted to kill Stan?" and thinking that maybe Stan had discovered something terrible at or about Positron and "was going to warn everyone. Could that be the reason they wanted him dead?" (183). She doesn't seem to question why they made *her* do the procedure, presumably believing that they meant to test her, as they said. As she prepares to depart for Stan's funeral, Aurora says they must wait for "a very special guest. He wanted to be here in person, to support you in your loss" (190). The mystery man turns out to be Ed, the head of Positron. Charmaine is flattered, but also wonders "*What does he want?*" (191, emphasis in original). She can tell, even in the car going to the funeral, that Ed is attracted to her because of the way he is looking at her with "reverence crossed with hidden lust, but behind that a determination to get what he wants" (198).

Charmaine forces herself to get through the funeral and subsequent reception; Aurora continues to accompany, or surveil, her. Soon Jocelyn appears at Charmaine's house to tell her that Stan isn't really dead and there is a plan to get her out of Positron to join him. Jocelyn also shares the information that Ed is having a sexbot made with her face on it but that "once he's practiced on that he'll want the real thing" (213). What they want Charmaine to do is to get close to Ed in order to spy on him. Jocelyn is clear, however, that she is not to actually have sex with Ed, "so he thinks you're modest. That's part of his obsession with you: so hard to find a modest girl these days" (213). Ed makes her assignment easy by beginning to court her, continuing to act on the interest he showed at Stan's staged funeral. In one of their dinners out, Charmaine observes that "she's finding this date with Ed a little difficult. More than a little: she doesn't know how to play this, because it's unclear what he wants, or not what: when" (221). During that same evening, Ed shares that "there are some doubts" about whether Stan died in the fire or "in a different way" (223). But he promises to "take care of that rumour for you" (223). Charmaine recognizes immediately that this is subtle blackmail, thinking that "you're bribing me! You know I killed Stan, you know I have to pretend he died saving chickens, and now you're twisting my arm" (223). However, she also thinks that "working in secret with Jocelyn like this—it was exciting in a way" (224). So, in an odd way, both Max / Phil and Jocelyn are providing her with new experiences and moments of enthusiasm or titillation.

Ed's next move is to transfer her from her job in the hospital to a job as his personal assistant, which turns out not to entail much actual work. She "sits at a desk outside Ed's office and does nothing much," but she is able to keep tabs on his calendar and whereabouts. Charmaine is surprised that he hasn't made another move on her or asked her out and is puzzled about why he even wants her as his assistant. Jocelyn clears that up: he wants her there "so nobody else can get you" (231). It's a territorial move, in a way, protecting the object he intends to make his. It's clear her needs and desires are not important.

The construction of the Charmaine sexbot is proceeding on schedule. Jocelyn shows her some surveillance film of Ed inspecting it. It looks exactly like her, and Charlene is both terrified and finds it "thrilling in a strange way" (232). In Ed's first encounter with the sexbot, once the beta version is finished, there is an accident. The bot "went into spasm, trapping Ed inside it, and then it started thrashing around" (236). Jocelyn is amused as she describes the end result: Ed "got a little bent out of shape" (235), clearly a euphemism for penile injury. Ed orders the sexbot destroyed and tells the technicians "he's through with substitutes" (236), a decision which puts Charmaine at risk. This could certainly simply be a plot twist to move the action along, but it does prompt the question of whether Atwood is offering subtle criticism of or warnings about the scientific advancements that enable the creation of humanlike robots and artificial intelligence.

Jocelyn tells Charmaine that Ed plans to take her to Vegas, where he intends to have her undergo an imprinting procedure, which will establish Ed as the object of her desire. Charmaine is horrified, thinking of what this means for her, but also what it means for Stan. Jocelyn describes what will happen as the result of the operation: "you'll come to when the operation's over, and there will be Ed, holding your hand and gazing into your eyes, and you'll take one look at him and throw your arms around him and say you'll love him forever. Then you'll beg him to make whatever sexual use of you he wants. And you'll mean that, every single word. You'll never get enough of him. That's how this thing is supposed to work" (264). This description embodies a prevailing myth that all men want is access to sex all the time; the implication here is that the woman a man desires must passionately provide sex, regardless of the mechanism that produces this result.

Jocelyn has been told by Ed to accompany Charmaine as her bodyguard to keep her safe, or perhaps to ensure that no other man interacts with her. Presumably this also means she will make sure the procedure doesn't happen. Once on the plane, Charmaine is curious about what's supposed to happen next. Ed has told Jocelyn to drug Charmaine's drink; Jocelyn will say she fainted and call for an ambulance and Charmaine will be taken to a clinic. When she starts to feel woozy after drinking some water, Charmaine immediately assumes that Jocelyn has double-crossed her. But she can't do anything about it; she passes out.

Back at Positron, Stan has awakened from the fake Special Procedure; he's alone and lying "in a large bin filled with knitted blue teddy bears" (157), the kind Charmaine's prison knitting group has been producing. He quickly discovers he's shackled to the bin, which he assumes "must be to keep him from wandering around" (158). Jocelyn arrives to share with him the next steps in her plan to get Stan out of the facility; she has adjusted the databank so that Stan will replace someone named Waldo who has died; she's changed the biometrics to ensure the replacement is seamless and unquestioned. He will be working "on a Possibilibots team" helping produce sex robots (165). When he was outside, "the guys down at the scooter depot" had shared rumors that "full production ha[d] begun on the new and improved sexbots that are in the trial stage somewhere in the depths of Positron" (108); we know this is true from Jocelyn's conversations with Charmaine. He will be helping manufacture them while he waits for someone to approach him with the password "Tiptoe Through the Tulips" (166).

His new teammates educate him about all the features, upgrades, and customization that are available on the sexbots. Stan learns that customers can even have a bot produced that has the face of an actual person; presumably male *or* female customers could order one, although so far only orders by men have been discussed. He is shocked to see a photo of Charmaine in Customization Plus, where the bots that are commissioned are created. He is unable to learn who commissioned the Charmaine bot. One of his coworkers, Budge, tells him that it's an "ultra-special order. We've been told to be very meticulous with it" (194). Budge then says, "we really have to tiptoe through the tulips on this one," surprising Stan, who thought earlier that "not one of the guys at lunch looks like the Tiptoe Through the Tulips kind" (177). In fact, Budge turns out to be part of the group of saboteurs attempting to take down the Positron Project. Budge was smuggled into the facility, in contrast to Stan who is being smuggled out disguised as an Elvis sexbot. Stan assumes it was Jocelyn who arranged for Budge's entry, but then discovers that his brother Conor is involved, which perhaps explains how Conor knew enough to warn him about the Positron Project earlier. Budge also tells him that Positron is experimenting with a disturbing procedure to "wipe out your previous love object and imprint you with a different one" (262); apparently these procedures are being done without consultation with the women, who simply "wake up" with this new attachment (204). Although generally love is thought of as a powerful, deeply felt emotion, the novel seems to imply that it, in addition to desire, can easily be altered—here by surgical manipulation.

Although in her novels, Atwood seems agnostic about consensual paid sex work—after all, in *The Year of the Flood*, sex worker Ren is one of her protagonists—in *The Heart Goes Last*, she offers an implicit critique of this particular commodification of sexual desire, extending her critique of the unethical overreach of scientists. The sexbots purport to offer a way to experience and act on sexual desire without human connection, thus rendering other people unnecessary and invisible. The bots can be requisitioned by either men or women and are infinitely customizable; they can be created to meet the needs of any sexual orientation or sexual fetish. The imprinting process is equally problematic. Not only is it performed on people without their knowledge or consent, but the result of the process also renders the victims devoid of agency. In the situations of both the sexbots and the imprinting victims, we see patriarchal science deployed to create objectified bodies to serve the sexual desires of (primarily) men. In some ways, it is reminiscent of the handmaids in *The Handmaid's Tale* whose sole purpose is to be a receptacle for the Commanders' semen and an incubator for their babies, although desire is supposed to be irrelevant to that process.

Stan is assigned a guide to help him. The guide turns out to be Veronica, one of the former prostitutes from Dust. She has undergone the imprinting procedure herself, but it went awry, and she imprinted on a blue knitted teddy bear instead of the man who had ordered the procedure. Later in the novel, Ed tells some of his investors that he didn't "know what saboteur gave her that bear. . . . The guy who ordered the . . . operation was very annoyed when he turned up, but he was too late. She'd already imprinted" (263). Veronica has made her peace with it, happily observing that she "can take my loved one with me everywhere I go" (209). What this means for her becomes obvious to Stan on their journey as he has to listen to her "making out with the blue knitted bear" (228). In a humorous and totally ridiculous way, Veronica's desire for a stuffed animal illuminates the absurdity of the imprinting process.

The timetable for getting Stan out has escalated as "IT has discovered that some crucial files have been copied" and these are what is "on the flashdrive he will be smuggling out" (214). Veronica and Stan have to leave before there is a search for the missing data. Conveniently, an order of Elvis sexbots is being shipped to Vegas that night and Stan will be one of them, in a shipping crate that's been outfitted with discreet airholes. Stan dons an Elvis costume; the flashdrive is hidden in the Elvis belt buckle. Veronica is posing as a Marilyn Monroe sexbot; she'll be smuggled out with him so she can assist him when they reach their destination. Veronica gives him some sedatives to calm him, and he fades in and out during the journey, alternating lucid moments with terrifying nightmares. When he awakens, he's surrounded by other fake Elvises, who, he quickly realizes are "all gay" (238). He worries about how to "tell them he's as straight as a Kansas highway without sounding rude" (238), apparently assuming that otherwise they would make a move on him, thus unfortunately articulating a homophobic belief held by many that gay people hit on others indiscriminately.

But for Atwood's authorial skill, *The Heart Goes Last* might devolve into slapstick comedy, and there is some leaning into that genre. However, her careful character portrayals and plot sequencing works to preclude it. Still, Stan does ask himself at one point "why can't life hand him something plausible for a change?" (271); the reader might ask the same question about the plausibility of this plot. It is impossible not to be curious about what is coming next, though.

The other Elvises coach Stan about how to hide in plain sight, by acting like Elvis. He can choose his UR-ELF Elvis specialty from "singing Elvis . . . Wedding Elvis . . . Escort Elvis . . . Chauffeur Elvis . . . Bodyguard Elvis . . . [or] Retirement Home Elvis" (238–39). He is assigned to gigs at retirement homes, primarily to deliver flowers to elderly women residents in his Elvis persona. Although he at first finds the whole thing ludicrous, he finds that "the more he does it, the easier it becomes" and he takes pleasure in providing "such joy" to the women, many of whom are in the final stages of life (243). Other than their performances, the Elvises live a relatively normal life, eating, drinking, playing cards and otherwise passing the time. It turns out that, in fact, the Elvises are not all gay, but the clients "prefer the Elvises to be gay" (248). This way, there is no "uninvited hanky-panky" (249). Most of them are out-of-work actors. Here Atwood slips in a reference to another Shakespeare play based on *Midsummer Night's Dream* and retooled as *Midsummer Night's Scream*. Some Elvises are missing from the group because they've been cast in that show.

Now that Stan is accustomed to his nursing home appearances, the other Elvises want to book him as Escort Elvis for a big convention that's coming to town. It sounds like an easy gig: "see a show, eat some food, drink some booze" (250). But it turns out that some of the customers might also want "sex-for-cash," to which Stan has an immediate objection (250). He is quickly reassured that, in fact, an Elvis sexbot will be provided in his place. He only has to wait in the lobby with an earpiece in case there is some problem with the bot. This doesn't sound particularly appealing to Stan, who thinks how unappealing it will be to be "eavesdropping while some mildewed hen has an orgasm" (250). Stan often thinks of women in negative or contemptuous terms, and this is one of those moments, presumably part of why Shirm objects to his attitudes about women ("*The Heart Goes Last*"). His assignment for the convention is a woman who "wants someone to take her to a show" (257). One of the other Elvises, Rob, coaches Stan on how to be an attentive escort; he should "compliment them on their dress. Gaze into their eyes. All of that" (257), instructions which send a message about the credulousness of women. Still, presumably a woman who would hire an Elvis escort expects to be courted and is aware of the performativity.

Stan gets an unpleasant shock when, returning from an outing on the Strip, he learns that four men were looking for him; they have a copy of Stan and Charmaine's honeymoon picture. Although he's worried and fearful, he has to go meet his client, who turns out to be Lucinda Quant, the television personality whose show Charmaine used to watch and whom Charmaine met when she was doing extra time in Positron. The show Lucinda has chosen is the Green Man Group, "a spinoff of the Blue Man Group" (267). One of the acts is "a tulip number, done to 'Tiptoe Through the Tulips'," which Stan immediately recognizes as his code from the Possibilibots interlude (267) and puts him on high alert.

After the show, Lucinda "expects Stan to take her to one of the bars in this joint and share a White Russian or two with him, and tell her his life story" (268). When she visits the ladies' room, Veronica—in her Marilyn costume—spirits him away; she tells him another Elvis will replace him. She escorts Stan back to the Green Man Group dressing room where he waits anxiously for whatever is about to happen next. He is taken off guard when Lucinda reappears. It turns out that she is actually his contact and is there to take delivery of the flashdrive sequestered in his belt buckle. She plans to break a major story by telling the truth about the Positron Project. Immediately thereafter, members of the Green Man Group appear who are actually Stan's brother Conor and his associates in disguise. Stan will join the Green Man Group which, Conor says is "the best cover while we're waiting to pull the job" (273). It turns out that Conor has been working with—or for—Jocelyn for some time and he knows to keep his mouth shut and not to "ask why she wants what she wants, that's her business" (273). Jocelyn has told Conor that Stan is crucial to the success of the job. The Green Man Group will perform at one of the nursing homes where they will "do the snatch" (274), although it's unclear at this point who they'll be snatching or why. Conor rehearses the plan with Stan: they will all continue to perform until they hear an ambulance arriving, at which point they will leave the stage to meet the ambulance. Once they do, Stan discovers that Charmaine and Ed are there, both unconscious.

Charmaine, Ed, and Jocelyn's husband Phil all undergo the imprinting surgery; now we see men imprinting on new love objects. Phil, now being referred to as Max again, imprints on Aurora; Jocelyn has already arranged for her divorce from him. This is the first time we have seen the imprinting process used on male subjects, but that does little to erase the creepiness of it. Stan is glued to Charmaine's bedside so that when she awakens, she will properly imprint on him, as she does, insisting on having sex immediately after waking up. Stan is ecstatic as "Charmaine loves him! She loves him again. She loves him more than before" (288). Jocelyn has arranged for Ed to imprint on Lucinda; Lucinda plans to leave the country with him and go to Dubai, where there are "no questions asked" (290). There is also no extradition, so Ed is safe from prosecution. Stan is frustrated at this solution, asking Jocelyn, "why're you letting him [Ed] off so cheap? . . . After everything he did" (290). But Jocelyn has planned this carefully; Ed can't testify about Positron without implicating her and other backers of the project, including politicians. This ensures a lack of punishment or accountability for both her and them. Although the main goal was to shut down Positron and its illicit and dangerous activities, the fact that those who planned and benefited from the project will go free with no consequences echoes uncomfortably what is often seen after corporate malfeasance is discovered. If anyone at all is punished, it is often low-level actors while the powerful are protected from the repercussions of their decisions and actions.

Once the patients are released from the clinic, a group wedding is arranged: Aurora and Max and Ed and Lucinda are getting married; Charmaine and Stan are renewing their vows. Charmaine is delighted that "the dark part of herself that was with her for so long seems to be completely gone" (292). She is not without moral qualms though. She wonders if "loving Stan really count[s] if she can't help it? Is it right that the happiness of her married life should be due not to any special efforts on her part but to a brain operation she didn't even agree to have?" (294), and she questions whether what she thinks she feels is authentic and real. What's also not clear is why Charmaine had to undergo the procedure at all. Presumably once she was free from Ed and discovered Stan was alive and back in her life, they could have found a way to rebuild their marriage and make peace with their joint infidelities without the imprinting procedure being necessary.

Lucinda Quant breaks the Positron exposé on national news. She's completely convincing as "she has extensive document trails and video footage" (284). Predictable public outrage follows. The lurid details captivate the public: "Prison abuses! Organ harvesting! Sex slaves created by neurosurgery! Plans to suck the blood of babies" (285). Deeper questions are also asked: "the misappropriation of people's bodies, the violation of public trust, the destruction of human rights—how could such things have been allowed to happen?" (285). And there are predictable attempts to assign blame or responsibility: "Where was the oversight? Which politicians bought into this warped scheme in a misguided attempt to create jobs and save money for the taxpayer?" (285). Such reactions are not unexpected although the language is overly dramatic and sensationalized, as such news coverage often is.

Still, the outrage has barely cooled when the "there's always two sides, at least two sides" (285) rationalization begins. Some justify the organ harvesting because they "were criminals anyway, . . . this was a real way for them to pay their debt to society and make reparation for the harm they caused" (285), ignoring the lack of willingness or consent of those whose organs were harvested. Others argue that after Positron had run out of criminals, they were "snatching people off the street" (285) for the profits involved, using people who were guilty of nothing. Then, the argument offered is that perhaps the idea of Positron was actually positive because "who could sneeze at full employment and a home for everyone?" (285). Others respond that "these utopian schemes always went bad and turned into dictatorships" (285). These debates seem to leave open the possibility that such a scheme could be tried again in the future if the excesses and illegal behavior were curbed.

The ending of the novel is inconclusive; Ewa Kowal notes that there is no "uplifting happy ending, although Atwood ironically plays with the idea" ("Nostalgia, Kitsch" 150). Stan and Charmaine stay in Vegas, settle down, and have a baby; Charmaine hopes for a second one soon. Neither can really trust the other, although "they're evenly balanced on the teeter-totter of cheating, so by mutual consent they never mention it" (302). Although Jocelyn has lied to Stan, telling him that Charmaine knew about the plot to help him escape, he's not sure he believes it. Charmaine has some distrust of Stan as well and is "keeping an eye on Stan too, because she has this notion that he might ramble off and get involved in adventures, with or without predatory women" (302). Stan is having all the passionate sex he could want, discovering that, in addition to the operation on Charmaine's brain, when he replicates Max's "verbal turn-ons" she becomes "toffee in his hands" (302). He does have some slight uneasy feeling that "the routine has become slightly predictable, but it would be surly to complain" (302). One can imagine that having to replicate the sex scenes he was forced to enact with Jocelyn might feel problematic. Stan's reaction might also be Atwood's way of signaling that having access to never-ending sex might not actually be as satisfying as anticipated.

For Charmaine's part, she is uncomfortable because "she still does think about Max, from time to time. In that way. Which is odd, because those feelings about Max were supposed to have been wiped" (303). She wonders how she could have these thoughts and feelings after the procedure. And Charmaine is still in the position of needing to manage Stan's moods, although not to avoid or minimize his anger. Now she ignores any bad moods and refuses to engage with them "because when he's grumpy he won't have sex, and the sex, is amazing, way better than before; how can it not be, now that her brain's been reborn?" (304). "How can it not be" implies that she, too, is working to convince herself that she is happy and completely satisfied. The reader, too, begins to wonder about whether the procedure was actually successful. Yet Stan and Charmaine both seem invested in the life they've rebuilt and in their current relationship.

Several months later, Jocelyn comes to share some information, asking Charmaine first whether she wants it; she explains: "if you hear it, you'll be more free but less secure. If you don't hear it, you'll be more secure but less free" (305). This creates a no-win situation for Charmaine: she can choose to be either less secure or less free. Charmaine decides to hear the information and Jocelyn delivers a bombshell; she tells Charmaine that she never really had the imprinting operation at all. At first Charmaine doesn't believe Jocelyn but then begins to ponder what that could mean, feeling a new sense of possibility for her future that had been lacking before. She wonders if there might be "someone who isn't Stan, waiting for her in the future" (306), although it's hard to know what she thinks would happen to Stan and their baby if she abandoned them for another man—unless she is simply imagining another illicit affair. Thus, the final scene of domestic bliss is immediately complicated by uncertainty, as Charmaine now seems to have a new set of options. The novel hints at the unsettling implication that Charmaine might choose something other than to wallow in happy domesticity. Then Atwood injects even more uncertainty as Jocelyn says, "the world is all before you, where to choose" and Charmaine responds, "How do you mean?" (306). This implies that, in addition to another man or another affair, there might be an even wider array of choices available to her. These are the last words of the novel.

The lack of closure at the end of *The Heart Goes Last* replicates the unresolved endings of several of the novels discussed in this book. Is Atwood suggesting that a more decisive ending can occur only if different choices are made? Since many of her novels warn about the consequences if society continues on its current path, is she suggesting that we can, or should, take action to forestall those results? Is it simply a challenge to fatalism, insisting that human agency is the most important thing in determining the future? Or maybe it is some combination of all of these options.

Somacarrera observes that *The Heart Goes Last* deals "with the struggle between corporate power and individual freedom" ("Questions of Power," 42), a relevant contemporary concern. In Rano Ringo's and Jasmine Sharma's feminist analysis of the novel, they read it as an example of "feminist futurity," suggesting that "as the story advances, one could perceive the role and significance of the female characters destabilizing the technocratic patriarchal order" ("'Do Time Now,'" 76); this seems to give more agency than is warranted to Charmaine, at least. She and Stan seem like pawns in a larger plot of which they're not fully aware. Throughout the novel, Charmaine and Stan "are more acted upon than active" (Shirm, "*The Heart Goes Last*") and "become hapless bystanders in everything from their marriage to the larger story" (Robinson, "*The Heart Goes Last*"). Ringo and Sharma also claim that Charmaine "emerges as a strong-willed female character" and that she and Jocelyn "rebel against the phallic technocracy of Ed" ("'Do Time Now,'" 84). That seems like a huge overstatement. In fact, it's hard to interpret Charmaine's actions as choosing to conspire with Jocelyn to negatively impact Positron. When Jocelyn tells her the truth about Stan and asks her to spy on Ed, Charmaine does not agree willingly. Instead, Jocelyn coerces her by threatening to show Ed the video footage of Phil / Max and Charmaine / Jasmine having extramarital sex. It is, as Charmaine notes, "blackmail" (214). Megan Cannella suggests that the relationship between Jocelyn and Charmaine is a balance of power, that "neither woman has the upper hand; [because] neither can succeed on her own" ("Feminine Subterfuge," 20). Again, I would argue that, although Jocelyn certainly needs Charmaine, her need exists within already-existing asymmetrical power relations. Jocelyn obviously is in a position of greater power because she is the one who has knowledge of the entire plan; she is the one telling Charmaine what to do; and she is the one who orchestrates the fake imprinting procedure for Charmaine and ultimately discloses the truth. She is clearly in charge.

In *The Heart Goes Last*, Atwood has written an ambitious novel that never loses the thread of its complicated plot. Sections of the novel are certainly comical. But even though there are comic interludes, they never overshadow the deep philosophical questions about free will, the prison-industrial complex, surveillance practices, capitalism, abuse of science and technology, and love and desire that Atwood addresses throughout the novel. The themes portrayed in *The Heart Goes Last*, in fact, echo themes present in all the novels discussed in this volume, reflecting Atwood's continuing interest in silencing and voice; storytelling and narrative choice; oppression and resistance; corporate, political, and patriarchal power; and questions about the morality and ethics of unfettered scientific advancement. Many of the novels end with unanswered questions, uncertainty about what might happen next, or a lack of closure. Perhaps Atwood intends us to recognize our own responsibilities to take action to intervene in the problems and potential outcomes she raises in her literature. Regardless, in all of Atwood's novels, we see her skillfully addressing contemporary problems and creating deep, complex characters and plots that compel the reader to continue reading and seeking out her work.

NOTES

Chapter 1—Understanding Margaret Atwood

1. Hulu announced that there would be a fifth season of *The Handmaid's Tale* likely released in late 2022 (O'Malley, "The Handmaid's Tale Season 5"). Atwood had a cameo role in the first season's first episode, playing an Aunt.
2. See Beaumont and Holpuch, "How *The Handmaid's Tale* Dressed Protests across the World" and Speare-Cole, "People Across U.S. Wear 'Handmaid's Tale' Cloaks to Protest Amy Coney Barrett's Supreme Court Nomination" for just a few examples.
3. Margaret Atwood Society, https://atwoodsociety.org.
4. Green Policies, Margaretatwood.ca, http://margaretatwood.ca/green-policies/.
5. *Surfacing*, https://www.imdb.com/title/tt0088208/.
6. A privately published chapbook *Double Persephone* was published earlier, in 1961 (Howells, "The Critical Reception of Atwood's Works: A Chronological Survey," xviii).
7. Currently out of print but, as Levine-Keating notes, it is "available almost in its entirety in both the United States and Canadian editions of Atwood's *Selected Poems, 1965–1975*" ("Atwood's *You Are Happy*," 153).
8. A few days later, the *Toronto Star* published a rebuttal to DiManno's article, written by Florence Ashley ("You Can Say Woman"), who argued for the appropriateness of trans-inclusive language and noted that no one was banning anyone from using the word *woman*.
9. *The Handmaid's Tale* appears on syllabi in courses in Women's, Gender, and Sexuality Studies and in science fiction classes, often alongside Marge Piercy's *Woman on the Edge of Time* (1976); Piercy herself has referred to Atwood as "an extraordinarily good writer" ("Margaret Atwood"). I first read *The Handmaid's Tale* in a college literature class and since then have taught it successfully in both literature classes and classes in women's, gender, and sexuality studies.
10. A theatrical version of *The Penelopiad* premiered in Stratford-upon-Avon in 2007.

Chapter 2—*The Handmaid's Tale* and *The Testaments*

1. In developments that uncannily speak to this question, the former US President, Donald J. Trump, certainly made attempts in this direction.
2. During the writing of this book, a draft of the Supreme Court's ruling written for the *Dobbs v. Jackson* case was leaked. In the draft, it was clear that the court could potentially overturn the 1972 *Roe v. Wade* ruling by returning the decision about the legality of abortion to the states, many of which have anti-abortion laws on the books. In response, Atwood published an excerpt from *Burning Questions* in the *Guardian*, arguing that no one should force women to give birth as that is akin to enslavement

("'Enforced Childbirth is Slavery'"). In her *Atlantic* article, she wrote "theocratic dictatorships do not lie only in the distant past: There are a number of them on the planet today. What is to prevent the United States from becoming one of them?" ("I Invented Gilead"). The final result of that case was that *Roe* was, in fact, overturned.

3. In an unusual turn of events, Atwood shared the prize with Bernardine Evaristo and her novel *Girl, Woman, Other*.

Chapter 3—*The Penelopiad* and *Hag-Seed*

1. For other examples of twentieth and twenty-first century rearticulations of canonical works, see Lois Waisbrooker's *A Sex Revolution* or Meg Wolitzer's *The Uncoupling*, both retellings of *Lysistrata*; Hillary Jordan's *When She Woke*, a modern version of *The Scarlet Letter*; or Jean Rhys's *Wide Sargasso Sea*, which is a prequel to *Jane Eyre*.

2. A theatrical version of *The Penelopiad* premiered in Stratford-upon-Avon in 2007. Michael Billington calls it "an eye-assaulting spectacle" but notes that he prefers Atwood's novel as "a far more radical inversion of Homeric myth" ("The Penelopiad").

3. This jealousy is reminiscent of the antagonism Serena Joy shows to Offred in *The Handmaid's Tale*.

4. Atwood ends the novel with a short chapter summarizing the plot of *The Tempest* for those unfamiliar with it, although the novel is eminently readable even without the Shakespearean context.

5. Atwood notes that "Similar prison programmes do in fact exist, or have existed, in the UK, US and Italy as well as in Canada" (Atwood, "A Perfect Storm"). See, for example, Shakespeare Behind Bars, an organization which uses theater with "incarcerated, post-incarcerated, and at-risk communities, allowing them to develop life skills that will ensure their successful integration into society" (https://shakespearebehindbars.org/). The documentary *Shakespeare Behind Bars*, directed by Hank Rogerson and Jilann Spitzmiller, profiles one such program. *Shakespeare Behind Bars: The Power of Drama in a Women's Prison* by Jean Trounstine describes a similar program in a women's prison.

Chapter 4—The *MaddAddam* Trilogy

1. Named after "an African antelope," as Ingersoll notes ("Survival in Margaret Atwood's Novel *Oryx and Crake*," 175).

2. Atwood designed a unique experience for the book tour for *Year*. At each stop, she used local performers to mount a staged version of the book, including the Gardeners' hymns. The tour is chronicled in Ron Mann's documentary, *In the Wake of the Flood* (2010); the hymns are available on a CD (Atwood and Stoeber, *Hymns of the God's Gardeners: From the Year of the Flood*).

3. Margaret Atwood, "Intestinal Parasites."

BIBLIOGRAPHY

Works by Margaret Atwood

NOVELS

Alias Grace. Toronto: McClelland & Stewart, 1996. New York: Doubleday, 1996.

The Blind Assassin. Toronto: McClelland & Stewart, 1996. New York: Doubleday, 2000.

Bodily Harm. Toronto: McClelland & Stewart, 1981. New York: Simon & Schuster, 1981.

Cat's Eye. Toronto: McClelland & Stewart, 1988. New York: Doubleday, 1989.

The Edible Woman. Toronto: McClelland & Stewart, 1969. Boston: Atlantic Little-Brown, 1970.

Hag-Seed. London: Hogarth Shakespeare, 2016.

The Handmaid's Tale. Toronto: McClelland & Stewart, 1985. Boston: Houghton Mifflin Company, 1986.

The Heart Goes Last. Toronto: McClelland & Stewart, 2015. New York: Doubleday, 2015.

Lady Oracle. Toronto: McClelland & Stewart, 1976. New York: Simon & Schuster, 1976.

Life Before Man. Toronto: McClelland & Stewart, 1979. New York: Simon & Schuster, 1980.

MaddAddam. Toronto: McClelland & Stewart, 2013. New York: Doubleday, 2013.

Oryx and Crake. Toronto: McClelland & Stewart, 2003. New York: Doubleday, 2001.

The Penelopiad: The Myth of Penelope and Odysseus. Edinburgh: Canongate Books, 2005.

The Robber Bride. Toronto: McClelland & Stewart, 1993. New York: Doubleday, 1993.

Surfacing. Toronto: McClelland & Stewart, 1972. New York: Simon & Schuster, 1973.

The Testaments. Toronto: McClelland & Stewart, 2019. New York: Doubleday, 2019.

The Year of the Flood. Toronto: McClelland & Stewart, 2009. New York: Doubleday, 2009.

SHORT FICTION

Bluebeard's Egg. Toronto: McClelland & Stewart, 1982. Boston: Houghton Mifflin Company, 1985.

Dancing Girls and Other Stories. Toronto: McClelland & Stewart, 1977, republished in 1982 and 1998.

Good Bones and Simple Murders. Toronto: Coach House Press, 1983.

Moral Disorder. Toronto: McClelland & Stewart, 2006. Boston: Doubleday, 2006.
Murder in the Dark. Toronto: Coach House Press, 1983.
My Evil Mother. Amazon Original Stories, 2022. Kindle and audiobook.
Stone Mattress. Toronto: McClelland & Stewart, 2014. Boston: Doubleday, 2014.
The Tent. Toronto: McClelland & Stewart, 2006. Boston: Doubleday, 2006.
Wilderness Tips. Toronto: McClelland & Stewart, 1991. Boston: Doubleday, 1991.

POETRY

The Animals in That Country. Don Mills, ON: Oxford University Press Canada, 1969.
The Circle Game. Bloomfield Heights, MI: Cranbrook Academy of Art, 1964.
Dearly: New Poems. New York: Ecco, 2021.
The Door. Boston: Houghton Mifflin Harcourt, 2007.
Double Persephone. Toronto: Hawkshead Press, 1961.
Eating Fire: Selected Poetry, 1965–1995. London: Virago Books, 1998.
Interlunar. Don Mills, ON: Oxford University Press Canada, 1984.
The Journals of Susanna Moodie. Don Mills, ON: Oxford University Press Canada, 1970.
Margaret Atwood Poems 1976–1986. London: Virago Books, 1991.
Morning in the Burned House. Toronto: McClelland & Stewart, 1995. Boston: Houghton Mifflin, 1995.
Power Politics. Toronto: House of Anansi Press, 1971.
Procedures for Underground. Don Mills, ON: Oxford University Press Canada, 1970.
Selected Poems. Don Mills, ON: Oxford University Press Canada, 1976.
Selected Poems: 1965–1975. Boston: Houghton Mifflin, 1976.
Selected Poems 1966–1984. Don Mills, ON: Oxford University Press Canada, 1990.
Selected Poems II: Poems Selected and New, 1976–1986. Don Mills, ON: Oxford University Press Canada, 1986.
Speeches for Dr. Frankenstein. Toronto: House of Anansi. Originally published in 1966; released as an e-book in 2012.
True Stories. Don Mills, ON: Oxford University Press Canada, 1981.
Two-Headed Poems. Don Mills, ON: Oxford University Press Canada, 1978.
You Are Happy. Don Mills, ON: Oxford University Press Canada, 1974.

GRAPHIC NOVELS

Angel Catbird. Milwaukie, OR: Dark Horse Comics, 2016
Angel Catbird: To Castle Catula. Milwaukie, OR: Dark Horse Comics, 2017.
Angel Catbird: The Catbird Roars. Milwaukie, OR: Dark Horse Comics, 2017.
The Handmaid's Tale. New York: Nan A. Talese, 2019.
War Bears #1. Milwaukie, OR: Dark Horse Comics, 2017.
War Bears #2. Milwaukie, OR: Dark Horse Comics, 2018.
War Bears #3. Milwaukie, OR: Dark Horse Comics, 2018.

CHILDREN'S LITERATURE

Anna's Pet (with Joyce Barkhouse). Toronto: James Lorimer & Co., 1980.
Bashful Bob and Doleful Dorinda. Toronto: Key Porter Books, 2004.
For the Birds. Madeira Park, BC: Douglas & McIntyre, 1990.
Princess Prunella and the Purple Peanut. Toronto: Key Porter Books, 1995.
Rude Ramsay and the Roaring Radishes. Toronto: Key Porter Books, 2003.

Up in the Tree. Toronto: McClelland & Stewart, 1978.
Wandering Wanda and Widow Wallop's Wunderground Washery. Toronto: McArthur, 2011.

SHORTER WORKS AND ESSAYS

Burning Questions: Essays and Occasional Pieces, 2004–2021. New York: Doubleday: 2022.
Curious Pursuits: Occasional Writing. London: Virago Books, 2005.
Days of the Rebels 1815–1840. Toronto: Natural Science of Canada, 1977.
In Other Worlds: SF and the Human Imagination. Toronto: McClelland & Stewart, 2011. New York: Doubleday, 2011.
Moving Targets: Writing with Intent, 1982–2004. Toronto: House of Anansi Press, 2004.
Negotiating with the Dead: A Writer on Writing. Cambridge: Cambridge University Press, 2002.
Payback: Debt and the Shadow Side of Wealth. Toronto: House of Anansi Press, 2008.
Second Words: Selected Critical Prose. Toronto: House of Anansi Press, 1982.
Strange Things: The Malevolent North in Canadian Literature. Don Mills, ON: Oxford University Press Canada, 2002.
Survival: A Thematic Guide to Canadian Literature. Toronto: House of Anansi Press, 1972.
Writing with Intent: Essays, Reviews, Personal Prose, 1983–2005. New York: Carroll & Graf, 2005.

OTHER WORKS BY MARGARET ATWOOD

"'Aliens Have Taken the Place of Angels': Margaret Atwood on Why We Need Science Fiction." Guardian, June 16, 2005. https://www.theguardian.com/film/2005/jun/17/.
"Am I a Bad Feminist?" Globe and Mail, January 13, 2018. https://www.theglobeandmail.com/opinion/.
"'Enforced Childbirth Is Slavery': Margaret Atwood on the Right to Abortion." Guardian, May 7, 2022. https://www.theguardian.com/us-news/2022/may/07/.
"The Handmaid's Tale and Oryx and Crake in Context." PMLA 119, no. 3 (May 2004): 513–17.
"Handmaid's Tale Characterized Unfairly by Its Opponents." San Antonio Express-News, April 12, 2006. https://freerepublic.com/focus/f-news/1613902/posts.
"Haunted by The Handmaid's Tale." Guardian, January 20, 2021. https://www.theguardian.com/books/2012/jan/20/.
"If You Can't Say Something Nice, Don't Say Anything at All." Saturday Night, January 6, 2001.
"An Interview with Margaret Atwood on Her Novel The Handmaid's Tale." https://www.penguinrandomhouse.com/books/6125/.
"Intestinal Parasites." margaretatwood.ca, n.d. http://margaretatwood.ca/books/.
"I Invented Gilead. The Supreme Court Is Making It real." The Atlantic, May 13, 2022.
 "Margaret Atwood: The Road to Ustopia." Guardian, October 14, 2011. https://www.theguardian.com/books/2011/oct/14/.
"The Myths Series and Me." Publishers Weekly, November 28, 2005. https://www.publishersweekly.com/pw/by-topic/columns-and-blogs/soapbox/.
"A Perfect Storm: Margaret Atwood on Rewriting Shakespeare's Tempest." Guardian, September 24, 2016. https://www.theguardian.com/books/2016/sep/24/.

"Spotty-Handed Villainesses: Problems of Female Bad Behaviour in the Creation of Literature." In Curious Pursuits: Occasional Writing. London: Virago Books, 2005.

Twitter post, October 19, 2021, 8:32 a.m. https://twitter.com/margaretatwood/status/.

"Ursula K Le Guin, by Margaret Atwood: 'One of the Literary Greats of the 20th Century.'" Guardian, January 24, 2018. https://www.theguardian.com/books/2018/jan/24/.

"What The Handmaid's Tale Means in the Age of Trump." New York Times, March 10, 2017. https://www.nytimes.com/2017/03/10/books/review/.

"Writing Utopia." In Curious Pursuits: Occasional Writing 1970–2006, 85–94. London: Virago Press, 2005.

Secondary Bibliography

Allardice, Lisa. "Margaret Atwood: 'I Am not a Prophet. Science Fiction Is Really about Now.'" *Guardian*, January 20, 2018. https://www.theguardian.com/books/2018/jan/20/.

Alter, Alexandra. "'I'm Too Old to Be Scared by Much': Margaret Atwood on Her *Handmaid's Tale* Sequel." *New York Times*, September 5, 2019. https://www.nytimes.com/2019/09/05/books/.

Anzaldúa, Gloria. *Borderlands/La Frontera: The New Mestiza*. San Francisco: Aunt Lute Press, 1987.

Armitstead, Claire. "It's a Culture War That's Totally out of Control': The Authors Whose Books Are Being Banned in US Schools." *Guardian*, March 22, 2022. https://www.theguardian.com/books/2022/mar/22/.

Ashley, Florence. "You Can Say Woman and We Can Say Person." *Toronto Star*, October 19, 2021. https://www.thestar.com/opinion/contributors/2021/10/19/.

"Atlantis Interview with Margaret Atwood." *Atlantis* 5, no. 2 (1980): 202–11.

Atwood, Margaret, and Orville Stoeber. *Hymns of the God's Gardeners*. Earthly Ark Music, 2009.

Atwood, Margaret, and Phyllida Lloyd. "She's Left Holding the Fort." *Guardian*, October 25, 2005. https://www.theguardian.com/stage/2005/oct/26/theatre.classics.

"Atwood on the Science Behind *Oryx and Crake*." Science Friday, n.d. https://www.sciencefriday.com/segments/.

Barber, John. "Atwood: 'Have I Ever Eaten Maggots? Perhaps. . . .'" *Globe and Mail*, September 11, 2009. https://www.theglobeandmail.com/arts/.

Beaumont, Peter, and Amanda Holpuch. "How The Handmaid's Tale Dressed Protests across the World." *Guardian*, August 3, 2018. https://www.theguardian.com/world/2018/aug/03/.

Bennett, Donna, and Nathalie Cooke. "A Feminist by Another Name: Atwood and the Canadian Canon." In *Approaches to Teaching Atwood's The Handmaid's Tale and Other Works*, edited by Sharon R. Wilson, Thomas B. Friedman, and Shannon Hengen, 33–42. New York: The Modern Language Association of America, 1996.

Birkerts, Sven. "Present at the Re-Creation." *New York Times*, May 18, 2003. https://www.nytimes.com/2003/05/18/books/.

Billington, Michael. "The Penelopiad." *Guardian*, August 3, 2007. https://www.theguardian.com/stage/2007/aug/03/theatre.margaretatwood.

Bland, Jared, "It's 'Scary' Watching Aspects of Her Fiction Come to Life, Margaret Atwood Says." *Globe and Mail*, August 24, 2013. https://www.theglobeandmail.com/arts/.

BIBLIOGRAPHY

Bouson, J. Brooks. "On Margaret Atwood." In *Critical Insights: Margaret Atwood*, edited by J. Brooks Bouson, 3–24. Ipswich, MA: Salem Press, 2013.

Boyd, Shelley. "Utopian Breakfasts: Margaret Atwood's *MaddAddam*." *Utopian Studies* 26, no. 1 (2015): 160–81.

Brall, Susan. "Theatre Review: 'The Nurse Antigone' by Theater of War Productions." *MD Theatre Guide*, March 20, 2022. https://mdtheatreguide.com/2022/03/.

Braund, Susanna. "'We're Here Too, the Ones without Names.' A Study of Female Voices as Imagined by Margaret Atwood, Carol Ann Duffy, and Marguerite Yourcenar." *Classical Receptions Journal* 4, no. 2 (2012): 190–208.

Bresge, Adina. "Margaret Atwood Worries More about the Fate of the Living than Her Legacy." *Toronto Star*, March 10, 2022. https://www.thestar.com/entertainment/books/2022/03/10/.

Byrd, Merry Lynn. "Maybe the Answer Was Miranda All Along: Margaret Atwood's *Hag-Seed* and Jacqueline Carey's *Miranda and Caliban*." *FemSpec* 18, no. 1 (2017): 75–80.

Cannella, Megan E. "Feminine Subterfuge in Margaret Atwood's *The Heart Goes Last*." In *Worlds Gone Awry: Essays on Dystopian Fiction*, edited by John J. Han, C. Clarke Triplett, and Ashley G. Anthony, 15–27. Jefferson, NC: McFarland, 2018.

Clay, Carolyn. "Grave New World." *The Providence Phoenix*, March 26, 2004.

Conroy, Catherine. "Margaret Atwood: 'When Did It Become the Norm to Expect a Porn Star on the First Date?'" *Irish Times*, March 1, 2018. https://www.irishtimes.com/culture/books/.

"Darkness and Light: Margaret Atwood Brings Her Dystopic Trilogy to a Dazzling Close." *The Economist*, September 16, 2013.

DiManno, Rosie. "Why Can't We Say 'Woman' Anymore?" *The Toronto Star*, October 15, 2021. https://www.thestar.com/opinion/star-columnists/2021/10/15/.

Dove-Viebahn, Aviva. "True to Life." *Ms. Magazine*, Winter 2020, 40–41.

Doyle, Sady. "Dystopia, for the 'Lulz.'" *In These Times*, August 22, 2013.

Dudding, Adam. "Margaret Atwood: The World Is Very Upsetting." *Stuff*, December 15, 2019. https://www.stuff.co.nz/entertainment/books/.

Dutkiewicz, Jan. "MaddAddam by Margaret Atwood." *Quill and Quire*, October 2013. https://quillandquire.com/review/maddaddam.

Evaristo, Bernardine. "The Year of the Flood." *Financial Times*, September 4, 2009. https://www.ft.com/content/.

Flood, Alison. "Margaret Atwood Wins Kitschies Red Tentacle Award for *The Heart Goes Last*." *Guardian*, March 8, 2016. https://www.theguardian.com/books/2016/mar/08/.

Fowles, Stacey May. "Review: Margaret Atwood's *The Heart Goes Last* Is Deeply Witty and Oddly Beautiful." *Globe and Mail*, September 25, 2015. https://www.theglobeandmail.com/arts/books-and-media/.

Freeman, Hadley. "Playing with Fire: Margaret Atwood on Feminism, Culture Wars and Speaking Her Mind." *Guardian*, February 19, 2022. https://www.theguardian.com/books/ng-interactive/2022/feb/19/.

Friedan, Betty. *The Feminine Mystique*. New York: W. W. Norton, 1963.

Friedman, Thomas B., and Shannon Hengen. "Materials." In *Approaches to Teaching Atwood's The Handmaid's Tale and Other Works*, edited by Sharon R. Wilson, Thomas B. Friedman, and Shannon Hengen, 7–20. New York: The Modern Language Association of America, 1996.

Gay, Roxane. *Bad Feminist*. New York: Harper Perennial, 2014.

Geek's Guide to the Galaxy. "Interview: Margaret Atwood." lightspeedmagazine.com, December 2013, 43. https://www.lightspeedmagazine.com/nonfiction/.

Gilbert, Sophie. "Margaret Atwood Bears Witness." *The Atlantic*, December 2019. https://www.theatlantic.com/magazine/archive/2019/12/.

———. "The Challenge of Margaret Atwood." *The Atlantic*, September 5, 2019. https://www.theatlantic.com/entertainment/archive/2019/09/.

Groskop, Viv. "*Hag-Seed* Review—Margaret Atwood Turns the Tempest into a Perfect Storm." *Guardian*, October 16, 2016. https://www.theguardian.com/books/2016/oct/16/.

Hansen, Elaine Tuttle. "Mothers Tomorrow and Mothers Yesterday, but Never Mothers Today: *Woman on the Edge of Time* and *The Handmaid's Tale*." In *Narrating Mothers: Theorizing Maternal Subjectivities*, edited by Brenda O. Daly and Maureen T. Reddy, 21–43. Knoxville: University of Tennessee Press, 1991.

Harrison, M. John. "*The Heart Goes Last* by Margaret Atwood Review—Rewardingly Strange." *Guardian*, September 23, 2015. https://www.theguardian.com/books/2015/sep/23/.

Hishon, Kerry. "Exploring the Greek Chorus." Theatrefolk, May 2, 2016. https://www.theatrefolk.com/blog/.

Howells, Coral Ann. "Introduction." In *The Cambridge Companion to Margaret Atwood*, 2nd ed., 4–13. Cambridge: Cambridge University Press, 2021.

———. "True Trash: Genre Fiction Revisited in Margaret Atwood's *Stone Mattress*, *The Heart Goes Last*, and *Hag-Seed*." *Contemporary Women's Writing* 11, no. 3 (December 2017): 297–314.

———. "The Critical Reception of Atwood's Works: A Chronological Survey." In *Critical Insights: Margaret Atwood*, edited by J. Brooks Bouson, 54–73. Ipswich, MA: Salem Press, 2013.

Ingersoll, Earl G. "Survival in Margaret Atwood's Novel *Oryx and Crake*." *Extrapolation* 45, no. 2 (2004): 162–75.

Isen, Tajja, and Daniel Viola. "The Making of Margaret Atwood," in *Margaret Atwood Studies* 14 (2021): 152–58.

Italie, Hillel. "Margaret Atwood Attempts to Torch Unburnable, $130,000 'Handmaid's Tale' Book with Flamethrower." *USA Today*, May 22, 2022. https://www.usatoday.com/story/entertainment/books/2022/05/24/.

Jameson, Fredric. "Then You Are Them." *London Review of Books* 31, no. 17 (September 10, 2009). https://www.lrb.co.uk/the-paper/v31/n17/.

Johnson, Mat. "Margaret Atwood's *The Heart Goes Last*." *New York Times*, September 23, 2015. https://www.nytimes.com/2015/09/27/books/review/.

Jordan, Hillary. *When She Woke*. Chapel Hill, NC: Algonquin Books, 2011.

Kadar, Marlene. "*The Journals of Susanna Moodie* as Life Writing." In *Approaches to Teaching Atwood's The Handmaid's Tale and Other Works*, edited by Sharon R. Wilson, Thomas B. Friedman, and Shannon Hengen, 146–52. New York: The Modern Language Association of America, 1996.

Kakutani, Michiko. "The Handmaid's Thriller: In *The Testaments*, There's a Spy in Gilead." *New York Times*, September 3, 2019. https://www.nytimes.com/2019/09/03/books/review/.

———. "A Familiar Cast of Fighters in a Final Battle for the Soul of the Earth."

BIBLIOGRAPHY

New York Times, September 14, 2009. https://www.nytimes.com/2009/09/15/books/15kaku.html.

Kowal, Ewa. "Nostalgia, Kitsch and the Great Recession in Margaret Atwood's *The Heart Goes Last* and *Westworld* (Season 1)." *Brno Studies in English* 45, no. 1 (2019): 143–55.

Kuźnicki, Slawomir. *Margaret Atwood's Dystopian Fiction: Fire Is Being Eaten.* Newcastle upon Tyne, UK: Cambridge Scholars, 2017.

Lang, Nancy, and Peter Raymont, dir. *Margaret Atwood: A Word after a Word after a Word Is Power.* 2019. https://www.imdb.com/title/tt11197082/

Lee, Felicia. "Back to the Scary Future and the Best-Seller List." *New York Times,* September 21, 2009. https://www.nytimes.com/2009/09/22/books/22atwood.html.

Le Guin, Ursula K. "The Year of the Flood." *Guardian,* August 28, 2009.

Levine-Keating, Helane. "Atwood's *You Are Happy*: Power Politics, Gender Roles and the Transformation of Myth." In *Approaches to Teaching Atwood's The Handmaid's Tale and Other Works,* edited by Sharon R. Wilson, Thomas B. Friedman, and Shannon Hengen, 153–60. New York: The Modern Language Association of America, 1996.

Lewis, Martin. "*The Handmaid's Tale.*" SF Site. https://www.sfsite.com/11a/ht139.htm.

Loyd, Amy Grace. "Inside the Transgressive, Deliciously Dangerous Mind of Margaret Atwood." *Esquire,* September 24, 2019. https://www.esquire.com/entertainment/books/.

Lyall, Sarah. "Review: Margaret Atwood's *The Heart Goes Last* Conjures a Kinky Dystopia." *New York Times,* September 29, 2015.

MacPherson, Heidi Slettedahl. *The Cambridge Introduction to Margaret Atwood.* Cambridge: Cambridge University Press, 2010.

Mann, Ron, dir. *In the Wake of the Flood.* 2010. https://www.sphinxproductions.com/.

Mead, Rebecca. "Margaret Atwood, the Prophet of Dystopia." *New Yorker,* April 10, 2007. https://www.newyorker.com/magazine/2017/04/17/.

Morris, Mary. "The Art of Fiction: Margaret Atwood." *Paris Review* 117 (Winter 1990): 69–88.

"The New Science of Sex and Gender." *Scientific American,* September 1, 2017. https://www.scientificamerican.com/article/.

O'Malley, Kate. "The Handmaid's Tale Season 5: Release Date, Spoilers, Trailer, Cast and Plot." *Elle,* January 27, 2022. https://www.elle.com/uk/.

"Open Counter-Letter: Steven Galloway Case at UBC." Accessed December 28, 2020, https://sites.google.com/ualberta.ca/counterletter/home

"An Open Letter to UBC: Steven Galloway's Right to Due Process." UBC Accountable, November 14, 2016. http://www.ubcaccountable.com/open-letter/.

"Oryx and Crake." *Kirkus Reviews,* May 6, 2003. https://www.kirkusreviews.com/book-reviews/.

Phillips, Emilia. "Three of Fiction's Brightest Stars Have New Books—of Poetry." *New York Times,* February 9, 2021. https://www.nytimes.com/2021/02/09/books/review/.

Piercy, Marge. "Margaret Atwood: Beyond Victimhood." *The American Poetry Review* 2, no. 6 (November–December 1973): 41–44.

Potts, Robert. "Light in the Wilderness." *Guardian,* April 26, 2003. https://www.theguardian.com/books/2003/apr/26/fiction.margaretatwood.

Pratt, Annis. "Surfacing and the Rebirth Journey." In *The Art of Margaret Atwood:*

Essays in Criticism, edited by Arnold E. Davidson and Cathy N. Davidson, 139–57. Toronto: House of Anansi Press, 1981.

Raftery, Deirdre. "Rebels with a Cause: Obedience, Resistance and Convent Life, 1800–1940." *History of Education: Journal of the History of Education Society* 42, no. 6 (2013): 729–44.

Rhys, Jean. *Wide Sargasso Sea*. New York: W.W. Norton, 1966.

Ringo, Rano, and Jasmine Sharma. "'Do Time Now, Buy Time for the Future': Phallic Deception and Techno-Sexual Agency in Margaret Atwood's *The Heart Goes Last*." *Messengers from the Stars: On Science Fiction and Fantasy* 4 (2019): 73–87.

Robinson, Tasha. "*The Heart Goes Last*: Imbeciles in the apocalypse," MPRNews, October 1, 2015. https://www.mprnews.org/story/2015/10/01/.

Rogerson, Hank, and Jilann Spitzmiller, dir. *Shakespeare Behind Bars*, 2006.

Rosenberg, Jerome. "Who Is This Woman?" In *Approaches to Teaching Atwood's The Handmaid's Tale and Other Works*, edited by Sharon R. Wilson, Thomas B. Friedman, and Shannon Hengen, 28–32. New York: The Modern Language Association of America, 1996.

Rousselot, Elodie. "Re-Writing Myth, Femininity, and Violence in Margaret Atwood's *The Penelopiad*," In *Myth and Violence in the Contemporary Female Text*, edited by V. G. Julie Ragan, 131–44. London: Routledge, 2011.

Rowling, J. K. "J. K. Rowling Writes about Her Reasons for Speaking out on Sex and Gender Issues." jkrowling.com. n. d. https://www.jkrowling.com/opinions/.

Salas, Gerardo Rodríguez. "'Close as a Kiss': The Challenge of the Maids' Gyn/Affection in Margaret Atwood's *The Penelopiad*." *Amaltea Revista de Mitocrítca* 7 (2015): 19–34.

"San Antonio Area School Board Reverses Ban on Handmaid's Tale." Chron, March 25, 2006. https://www.chron.com/news/houston-texas/article/.

Sawyer, Miranda. "Margaret Atwood: 'If You're Going to Speak Truth to Power, Make Sure It's the Truth.'" *Guardian*, September 12, 2020. https://www.theguardian.com/lifeandstyle/2020/sep/12/.

Sethi, Anita. "*The Heart Goes Last* by Margaret Atwood Review—Visceral Study of Desperation." *Guardian*, August 14, 2016. https://www.theguardian.com/books/2016/aug/14/.

Shakespeare, William. *The Tempest*, edited by Gerald Graff and James Phelan. New York: Bedford/St. Martin's Press, 2009.

Shastri, Sudha. "Revisi(ti)ng the Past: Feminist Concerns in Margaret Atwood's *The Penelopiad*." *Estudios de Mujeres* 6 (2008): 141–49.

Shirm, Gretchen. "*The Heart Goes Last*, by Margaret Atwood, Speculates on Life as a Prison." *Sydney Morning Herald*, September 18, 2015. https://www.smh.com.au/entertainment/books/.

Showalter, Elaine. "The Snowman Cometh." *London Review of Books*, May 2003. https://www.lrb.co.uk/the-paper/v25/n14/elaine-showalter/.

Snyder, Katherine V. "'Time to Go': The Post-apocalyptic and the Post-Traumatic in Margaret Atwood's *Oryx and Crake*." *Studies in the Novel* 43, no. 4 (Winter 2011): 470–89.

Somacarrera, Pilar. "Margaret Atwood on Questions of Power." In *The Cambridge Companion to Margaret Atwood*, 2nd ed., edited by Coral Ann Howells 32–46. Cambridge: Cambridge University Press, 2021.

BIBLIOGRAPHY

Speare-Cole, Rebecca. "People Across U.S. Wear 'Handmaid's Tale' Cloaks to Protest Amy Coney Barrett's Supreme Court Nomination." *Newsweek*, October 26, 2020. https://www.newsweek.com/.

Staines, David. "Margaret Atwood in Her Canadian Context." In *The Cambridge Companion to Margaret Atwood*, 2nd ed., edited by Coral Ann Howells 14–31. Cambridge: Cambridge University Press, 2021.

Stein, Karen. *Margaret Atwood Revisited*. Boston: Twayne Publishers, 1999.

———. "Surviving the Waterless Flood: Feminism and Ecofeminism in Margaret Atwood's *The Handmaids Tale, Oryx and Crake,* and *The Year of the Flood*." In *Critical Insights: Margaret Atwood*, edited by J. Brooks Bouson, 313–33. Hackensack, NJ: Salem Press, 2013.

St. John Mandel, Emily. "Brave New World." *New York Times*, October 30, 2016, A9.

Tolan, Fiona. "'I Could Say That, Too:' An Interview with Margaret Atwood." *Contemporary Women's Writing* 11, no. 2 (November 2017): 452–64.

———. *Margaret Atwood: Feminism and Fiction*. Amsterdam: Rodopi B.V., 2007.

Trounstine, Jean. *Shakespeare Behind Bars: The Power of Drama in a Women's Prison*. New York: St. Martin's Press, 2001.

Turner, Nick. "Margaret Atwood." British Council Literature. https://literature.britishcouncil.org/writer/.

VanSpanckeren, Kathryn. "The Trickster Text: Teaching Atwood's Works in Creative Writing Classes." In *Approaches to Teaching Atwood's The Handmaid's Tale and Other Works*, edited by Sharon R. Wilson, Thomas B. Friedman, and Shannon Hengen, 77–83. New York: The Modern Language Association of America, 1996.

Veshi on MSNBC. "Prolific Author Margaret Atwood Joins the #VelshiBannedBook Club." MSNBC, May 1, 2002. Video, 7 min, 25 sec. https://www.msnbc.com/velshi.

Vickroy, Laurie. "Sexual Trauma, Ethics, and the Reader in the Works of Margaret Atwood." In *Critical Insights: Margaret Atwood*, edited by J. Brooks Bouson, 254–75. Ipswich, MA: Salem Press, 2013.

Wagner, Erica. "'Writing Is Always an Act of Hope': Margaret Atwood on *The Testaments*." *New Statesman*, September 18, 2019. https://www.newstatesman.com/culture/2019/09/.

Waisbrooker, Lois. *A Sex Revolution*. Philadelphia: New Society Publishers, 1985. First published in 1893.

Wisker, Gina. *Margaret Atwood: An Introduction to Critical Views of Her Fiction*. New York: Palgrave MacMillan, 2012.

Wolitzer, Meg. *The Uncoupling*. New York: Riverhead Books, 2011.

Yeo, Debra. "Wayne McGregor-Margaret Atwood Ballet 'MADDADDAM' Will Finally Gets [sic] Its World Premiere in National Ballet of Canada's New Season." *The Toronto Star*, May 4, 2022. https://www.thestar.com/entertainment/stage/2022/05/04/.

York, Lorraine. *Margaret Atwood and the Labor of Literary Celebrity*. Toronto: University of Toronto Press, 2013.

Young, Robin. "'It's Creepily Similar': Margaret Atwood on *The Testaments* and the State of the U.S." WBUR, September 2, 2020. https://www.wbur.org/hereandnow/2020/09/02/.

Zajac, Paul Joseph. "Prisoners of Shakespeare: Trauma and Adaptation in Atwood's *Hag-Seed*." *Studies in the Novel* 52, no. 3 (Fall 2020): 324–43.

INDEX

AfterMeToo program, 12
Allardice, Lisa, 3
"Am I a Bad Feminist?" (Atwood), 12
Amnesty International, 15
Angel Catbird (Atwood), 10
Anzaldua, Gloria: *Borderlands/La Frontera*, 32
Aristophanes: *Lysistrata*, 106n1
Arthur C. Clarke Award, 17
Ashley, Florence: "You Can Say Woman," 105n8
Atwood, Margaret: on authors' portrayal of female characters, 32; awards received by, 1, 2–3, 5, 9, 17, 25, 84; on book bans, 13; childhood of, 1–2; on feminism, 10–12, 17; on fiction, 9; on gender, 12–13; on *Hag-Seed*, 42–44, 46; in *The Handmaid's Tale* TV series, 15, 105n1; on *MaddAddam* trilogy, 51, 52, 61; on myths, 34; on patriarchy and religion, 20, 28; on *The Penelopiad*, 34, 35; poetry of, 9; on politics, 25, 41; on power, 17, 26, 27, 33; short stories of, 9–10; and social media, 14–15; on speculative fiction, 61; on *The Tempest*, 42; on *The Testaments*, 25; on theater programs in prisons, 106n5
Atwood Gibson, Eleanor Jess, 2

Barber, John, 62
Bennett, Donna, 4, 10
Billington, Michael, 106n2
Birkets, Sven, 61
blackmail: in *Hag-Seed*, 48; in *The Heart Goes Last*, 83, 95, 103; in *MaddAddam*, 76; in *Oryx and Crake*, 56; in *The Year of the Flood*, 65
Bland, Jared, 14, 52, 82
Bodily Harm (Atwood), 3, 6–9
Booker Prize, 1, 2, 15, 25, 51, 61
Borderlands/La Frontera (Anzaldua), 32
Bouson, J. Brooks, 62
Boyd, Shelley, 70
Braund, Susanna, 34–35, 41
British Academy President's Medal, 2
Brontë, Charlotte: *Jane Eyre*, 106n1
Burning Questions (Atwood), 105n2
Byrd, Merry Lynn, 43, 47, 49

Canada: Atwood's criticism of, 3; Atwood's focus on, 10; in *Bodily Harm*, 7; in *The Handmaid's Tale*, 4, 18, 25, 33; in *Surfacing*, 5–6; in *The Testaments*, 4, 15, 29, 31, 33
Canongate Myths Series, 34
cautionary tales, 61, 103, 104
The Circle Game (Atwood), 9
Clay, Carolyn, 51
Conroy, Catherine, 12
Cooke, Nathalie, 4, 10
corporate practices, 3, 104; in *MaddAddam*, 76; in *Oryx and Crake*, 53–56, 64–66, 76; *The Year of the Flood*, 56, 64–66, 76

Dancing Girls and Other Stories (Atwood), 9
Dearly (Atwood), 9
DiManno, Rosie: "Why Can't We Say 'Women' Anymore?," 12–13

INDEX

Dobbs v. Jackson, 105n2
Double Persephone (Atwood), 105n6
Dove-Viebahn, Aviva, 27
Doyle, Sady, 52, 70, 75
dystopia, 13; in *The Handmaid's Tale*, 17; in *The Heart Goes Last*, 84; and *MaddAddam* trilogy, 51–52; in *The Year of the Flood*, 52

The Edible Woman (Atwood), 5
environmental devastation, 3; in *The Handmaid's Tale*, 18; in *Oryx and Crake*, 52, 53, 55
Evaristo, Bernardine, 82
execution: in *The Handmaid's Tale*, 22; in *MaddAddam*, 80; in *Oryx and Crake*, 54, 55; in *The Penelopiad*, 35, 39–41
extinction, 5, 15; in *Oryx and Crake*, 52–56

flashbacks. *See* memories
Fowles, Stacey May, 83, 86
Freeman, Hadley, 3, 13
Friedman, Thomas B., 3
Frye, Northrop, 2

Galloway, Steven, 11
gender: Atwood on, 12–13; in Atwood's work, 5, 6, 11; in *Hag-Seed*, 50; in *The Handmaid's Tale*, 19, 22, 23, 32–33; in *The Year of the Flood*, 63
Gibson, Graeme, 2, 5
Gilbert, Sophie, 25–27, 31, 36
Governor General's Award for Poetry, 9
Groskop, Viv, 42

Hag-Seed (Atwood): deception in, 34, 47; gender in, 44–45, 50; genres of, 42; hallucination in, 43, 45–50; male narrator in, 41; play-within-play in, 44, 46–49; plot of *The Tempest* summarized in, 106n4; power in, 42, 50; prison in, 42–50; as retelling of *The Tempest*, 15, 34, 43; revenge in, 43, 46, 48–49; *The Tempest* performed in, 44–47

The Handmaid's Tale (Atwood), 14; banning of, 13; Canada in, 4, 18, 25, 33; as cautionary tale, 61; characters of in *The Testaments*, 25–26; as dystopian, 17; execution in, 22; gender roles in, 19, 22, 23, 32–33; *Historical Notes* section of, 15, 23; jealousy in, 20, 21, 23, 32; memories in, 18–20, 22, 24, 27; patriarchy in, 15, 17, 19, 20, 28, 32–33, 97; power in, 21, 32, 33; relationships in, 19–22, 32; reproduction in, 17, 18, 20; resistance in, 19–20, 22–26; ritual in, 22; in school curriculum, 13, 105n9; sexual assault in, 22, 25; sex work in, 18, 20, 21; silencing in, 9; social status in, 19, 22; storytelling in, 23–26, 34, 35; surveillance in, 18, 19; survival in, 32–33; in United States, 4, 15, 17, 25; witness narratives in, 24–25
The Handmaid's Tale movie, 17
The Handmaid's Tale opera, 18
The Handmaid's Tale TV series, 1, 15, 17, 105n1
Hansen, Elaine Tuttle, 19
Harrison, M. John, 83–84
Harvard Arts medal, 2
Hawthorne, Nathaniel: *The Scarlet Letter*, 106n1
The Heart Goes Last (Atwood), 16, 83–84; betrayal in, 83, 87–90, 101–2; blackmail in, 83, 95, 103; dystopia/utopia in, 84, 85–87; euthanasia in, 90, 92–94; humor in, 83, 84, 98, 104; organ trafficking in, 83, 91, 101; power in, 92, 103–4; prison system in, 86, 87, 90–92, 100, 101, 104; relationships in, 84–85; resistance in, 83, 91–92, 96–100; science abused in, 91–92, 95–98, 100–101, 104; sex robots in, 83, 95–99, 101; sex work in, 85, 97; surveillance in, 83, 94–95, 104
Hengen, Shannon, 3
Hishon, Kelly, 35
Hitchens Prize, 2
Hogarth Shakespeare Project, 15, 41
Homer: *The Odyssey*, 15, 34, 36

INDEX

Howells, Coral Ann, 3–5, 42, 43, 49–50, 88

Ingersoll, Earl, 56, 61, 106n1
Isen, Tajia, 25

Jameson, Fredric, 52
Jane Eyre (Charlotte Brontë), 106n1
jealousy: in *The Handmaid's Tale*, 20, 21, 23, 32; in *MaddAddam*, 73–74; in *Oryx and Crake*, 53; in *The Penelopiad*, 37–38, 40
Johnson, Mat, 83
Jordan, Hillary: *When She Woke*, 106n1
The Journals of Susanna Moodie (Atwood), 9

Kadar, Marlene, 9
Kakutani, Michiko, 27, 31–32, 82
Kowal, Ewa, 101
Kuźnicki, Slawomir: on *The Handmaid's Tale*, 23, 24; on *MaddAddam* trilogy, 52, 54, 56, 62, 70, 77, 81

Lang, Nancy: *Margaret Atwood*, 1
Lee, Felicia R., 62
Le Guin, Ursula, 14, 57, 62
Life Before Man (Atwood), 5
Lloyd, Phyllida, 18
Loyd, Amy Grace, 25, 27
Lyall, Sarah, 83, 84, 89–90
Lysistrata (Aristophanes), 106n1

MacPherson, Heidi Slettedahl, 1, 10, 11, 52
"MADDADDAM" (McGregor), 51–52
MaddAddam (Atwood), 15, 16, 56; dystopia/utopia in, 51–52; humor in, 71–72; pigoons in, 73, 77–82; relationships in, 72–74, 77–79, 81, 82; storytelling in, 72, 74, 75, 79–81; survival in, 70, 74, 77, 78, 80–82; telepathy in, 71, 77, 79, 80; violence in, 70, 72, 75–76, 80
MaddAddam trilogy (Atwood), 54, 82, 92; Crakers in, 56–57; themes of, 5, 15–16, 51–52. *See also* individual titles

male narrative, 41, 61, 62
Man Booker Prize for Fiction. *See* Booker Prize
Margaret Atwood (Lang and Raymont), 1
Margaret Atwood Society, 2
Margaret Atwood Studies, 2
"Margaret Atwood: The Road to Ustopia" (Atwood), 17
McGregor, Wayne: "MADDADDAM," 51–52
Mead, Rebecca, 11
memories: in *The Handmaid's Tale*, 18–20, 22, 24, 27; in *The Heart Goes Last*, 84; in *MaddAddam*, 75–77; in *Oryx and Crake*, 15, 53, 61, 63; in *Surfacing*, 6; in *The Testaments*, 27; in *The Year of the Flood*, 63
#MeToo movement, 12
Miskimmon, Annilese, 18
Moodie, Susanna: *Roughing It in the Bush*, 9
Moving Targets (Atwood), 11
murder: in *Hag-Seed*, 48; in *MaddAddam*, 72, 76, 80; in *Oryx and Crake*, 55, 58–59; in *The Testaments*, 29; in *The Year of the Flood*, 69
mythology, 5, 9, 34–35

Nature Canada Douglas H. Pimlott Award, 5
The Nurse Antigone, 15

The Odyssey (Homer), 15, 34, 36
Orange Prize for Fiction, 61
Order of the Companions of Honour, 2–3
Oryx and Crake (Atwood), 11, 14, 15, 51; bioengineering in, 52–57, 61; as cautionary tale, 61; characters from in *The Year of the Flood*, 65, 68–70; corporate practices in, 53–56, 64, 65–66, 76; Crakers in, 52, 56–60, 77; extinction in, 52–56; and male narration, 41, 61, 62; memories in, 15, 53, 61, 63; murder in, 55, 58–59; pandemic in, 52, 53, 58–59; pigoons

Oryx and Crake (continued)
in, 53, 54, 59, 77–78; relationships in, 57–59; reproduction in, 56–57; resistance in, 54, 55; ritual in, 60, 72, 77; storytelling in, 52–53, 59, 61
O. W. Toad, 2, 5

Pachter, Charles, 9
patriarchy, 10, 104; in *The Handmaid's Tale*, 15, 17, 19, 20, 28, 32–33, 97; in *The Heart Goes Last*, 97; in *The Penelopiad*, 37, 40; and religion, 20, 28; in *The Testaments*, 28
PEN America, 13
PEN Center USA Lifetime Achievement Award, 2
The Penelopiad (Atwood): deception in, 34, 36; execution in, 35, 39–41; feminine narrative in, 34–35, 41; Helen of Troy in, 36–38, 40; jealousy in, 37–38, 40; marriage in, 36–39; and mythology, 5, 34–35; Odysseus in, 15, 36–41; as retelling of *The Odyssey*, 15, 34; storytelling in, 35–36; theatrical version of, 105n10, 106n2; truth in, 34–36, 39–41
PEN International, 15
Phillips, Emilia, 9
Piercy, Marge, 4; *Woman on the Edge of Time*, 105n9
Polk, Jim, 2
Portland Arts and Lectures series, 14
"Positron" (Atwood), 83
Potts, Robert, 52
power, 3, 15; Atwood on, 17, 26, 27, 33; in *Hag-Seed*, 42, 50; in *The Handmaid's Tale*, 21, 32, 33; in *The Heart Goes Last*, 92, 103–4; in *The Penelopiad*, 36, 38; in *The Testaments*, 25–26, 29–33
Pratt, Annis, 5
prison system: in *Hag-Seed*, 15, 42–50; in *The Heart Goes Last*, 86, 87, 90–92, 100, 101, 104; theater programs in, 106n5
protests: in *The Heart Goes Last*, 91; in *The Testaments*, 29; and use of *The Handmaid's Tale* wardrobe, 1, 18

Radcliffe College, 2
Raftery, Deirdre, 28
Raymont, Peter: *Margaret Atwood*, 1
Red Tentacle award, 84
relationships, 5–8; in Hag Seed, 43, 50; in *The Handmaid's Tale*, 20–22, 32; in *The Heart Goes Last*, 84–85; in *MaddAddam*, 72–74, 77–79, 81, 82; in *Oryx and Crake*, 57–59; in *The Penelopiad*, 36–40; in *The Year of the Flood*, 72
religion: in *The Handmaid's Tale*, 20, 28; in *The Testaments*, 26, 28; in *The Year of the Flood*, 62, 64
reproduction, 105n2; in *The Handmaid's Tale*, 17, 18, 20; in *Oryx and Crake*, 56–57
resistance, 3, 104; in *The Handmaid's Tale*, 19–20, 22–26; in *The Heart Goes Last*, 83, 91–92, 96–100; in *Oryx and Crake*, 54, 55; in *The Testaments*, 26, 28–31; in *The Year of the Flood*, 64
revenge, 15; in *Hag-Seed*, 43, 46, 48–49; in *MaddAddam*, 75–76
Rhys, Jean: *Wide Sargasso Sea*, 106n1
Ringo, Rano, 103
ritual: in *The Handmaid's Tale*, 22; in *MaddAddam*, 72; in *Oryx and Crake*, 60, 72, 77; in *The Year of the Flood*, 67–68, 70
The Robber Bridegroom (Atwood), 5
Roe v. Wade, 105n2
Rogerson, Hank: *Shakespeare Behind Bars*, 106n5
Rosenberg, Jerome, 4
Roughing It in the Bush (Moodie), 9
Rousselot, Elodie, 34, 35, 39, 40
Rowling, J. K., 12
Royal Society of Canada, 3
Ruders, Poul, 18

Salas, Gerardo Rodríguez, 35, 37
Sawyer, Miranda, 11
The Scarlet Letter (Hawthorne), 106n1
science, 3; abuse of in *The Heart Goes Last*, 91–92, 95–98, 100–101, 104; in *Oryx and Crake*, 52, 53, 56, 61

INDEX

science fiction, 13–14
Selected Poems (Atwood), 105n7
Sethi, Anita, 84, 90
sex: in *The Handmaid's Tale*, 20–21; in *The Heart Goes Last*, 87–90, 94, 102
A Sex Revolution (Waisbrooker), 106n1
sexual assault: in *MaddAddam*, 70, 78; in *The Handmaid's Tale*, 22, 25; in *The Penelopiad*, 39–41; in *The Year of the Flood*, 63, 69, 70
sex work: in *The Handmaid's Tale*, 18, 20, 21; in *The Heart Goes Last*, 85, 97; in *Oryx and Crake*, 57; in *The Year of the Flood*, 63, 68, 97
Shakespeare, William: *The Tempest*, 15, 34, 41–47, 49, 50, 106n4
Shakespeare Behind Bars, 106n5
Shakespeare Behind Bars (Rogerson and Spitzmiller), 106n5
Shakespeare Behind Bars (Trounstine), 106n5
Sharma, Jasmine, 103
Shastri, Sudha, 41
Shirm, Gretchen, 84, 99
Showalter, Elaine, 52, 56
Snyder, Katherine V., 52–53
Somacarrera, Pilar, 9, 103
speculative fiction, 13–14, 61
Spitzmiller, Jilann: *Shakespeare Behind Bars*, 106n5
"Spotty-Handed Villainesses" (Atwood), 32
Staines, David, 2, 3, 6–8, 42
Stein, Karen: on *Bodily Harm*, 7; on *MaddAddam* trilogy, 57, 61–62, 64, 82; on storytelling in Atwood's work, 5; on *Surfacing*, 4, 5–6
St. John Mandel, Emily, 44, 46–47, 49
storytelling, 104; in Atwood's work, 3, 5; in *The Handmaid's Tale*, 23–26, 34, 35; in *MaddAddam*, 72, 74, 75, 79–81; in *Oryx and Crake*, 52–53, 59, 61; in *The Penelopiad*, 35–36; in *The Testaments*, 26, 34
Surfacing (Atwood), 4–7
surveillance, 16; in *The Handmaid's Tale*, 18, 19; in *The Heart Goes Last*, 83, 94–95, 104

survival, 4, 5; in *The Handmaid's Tale*, 32–33; in *MaddAddam*, 70, 74, 77, 78, 80–82; in *Oryx and Crake*, 52–53; in *The Testaments*, 26–27
Survival (Atwood), 3, 4
sustainability, 3, 5; in *The Year of the Flood*, 5, 62, 64, 69–70

telepathy: in *MaddAddam*, 71, 77, 79, 80; in *Oryx and Crake*, 60
The Tempest (Shakespeare), 15, 34, 41–47, 49, 50, 106n4
The Testaments (Atwood), 1; characters from *The Handmaid's Tale* in, 25–26; narration in, 25–27, 34; power in, 25–26, 29–33; resistance in, 26, 28–31; silencing in, 9; survival in, 26–27; United States in, 4, 15; witness narratives in, 26, 31–32, 35
The Testaments TV series, 25
theocratic dictatorships, 105–6n2
Thomas Fisher Rare Book Library, 14
Tolan, Fiona: on *The Handmaid's Tale*, 17, 24, 25; on *Oryx and Crake*, 53, 57, 58, 60–61
transphobia, 12–13, 105n8
Trounstine, Jean: *Shakespeare Behind Bars*, 106n5
Trump, Donald J., 33, 105n1
Turner, Nick, 61

The Uncoupling (Wolitzer), 106n1
United States: Atwood on, 17, 33, 105–6n2; in *The Handmaid's Tale*, 4, 15, 17, 25; negative portrayals of, 3; in *The Testaments*, 4, 15
University of Toronto's Victoria College, 2
ustopia, 14
utopia, 13; in *The Heart Goes Last*, 86–87; and *MaddAddam* trilogy, 52; in *The Year of the Flood*, 52

VanSpanckeren, Kathryn, 23
Vickroy, Laurie, 63
Viola, Daniel, 25
violence: in *The Heart Goes Last*, 84; in *MaddAddam*, 70, 72, 75–76; in *Oryx*

violence (*continued*)
and *Crake*, 54; in *The Testaments*, 26; in *The Year of the Flood*, 63, 66, 68–69

Wachtel, Eleanor, 9
Wagner, Erica, 17
Waisbrooker, Lois: *A Sex Revolution*, 106n1
War Bears (Atwood), 1, 10
When She Woke (Jordan), 106n1
"Why Can't We Say 'Women' Anymore?" (DiManno), 12–13
Wide Sargasso Sea (Rhys), 106n1
Wilderness Tips (Atwood), 4–5
Wisker, Gina: on Atwood, 1, 3, 4; on *The Handmaid's Tale*, 19, 24, 25; on *MaddAddam*, 82; on *Oryx and Crake*, 52; on *The Penelopiad*, 35
witness narratives: in *The Handmaid's Tale*, 24–25; in *The Penelopiad*, 35, 36; in *The Testaments*, 26, 31–32, 35
Wolitzer, Meg: *The Uncoupling*, 106n1

Woman on the Edge of Time (Piercy), 105n9

The Year of the Flood (Atwood), 14–16, 51; abduction in, 65–66, 69; book tour for, 106n2; and characters from *Oryx and Crake*, 65, 68–70; corporate practices in, 56, 64–66, 76; dystopia/utopia in, 52; *MaddAddam* Grandmasters in, 66, 68, 69; pandemic in, 63, 67, 68; pigoons in, 67, 78; relationships in, 72; religion in, 62, 64; ritual in, 67–68, 70; sex work in, 63, 68, 97; social order in, 61–62; sustainability in, 5, 62, 64, 69–70; violence in, 63, 66, 68–69
York, Lorraine, 2, 5, 23, 24
You Are Happy (Atwood), 9, 105n7
"You Can Say Woman" (Ashley), 105n8
Young, Robin, 25

Zajac, Paul Joseph, 41–44, 49